The Sculpture of Thailand

HIS MAJESTY KING BHŪMIBOL ADULYADEJ
AND HER MAJESTY QUEEN SIRIKIT OF THAILAND
HAVE GRACIOUSLY CONSENTED TO ACT AS
PATRONS OF THIS EXHIBITION.

Asia House Gallery, New York City
The Cleveland Museum of Art, Cleveland, Ohio
Indiana University Art Museum, Bloomington, Indiana
The Montreal Museum of Fine Arts, Montreal, Canada
Seattle Art Museum, Seattle, Washington
Dallas Museum of Fine Arts, Dallas, Texas

The Sculpture of Thailand

THEODORE BOWIE, editor

M. C. SUBHADRADIS DISKUL

A. B. GRISWOLD

Photographs by BRIAN BRAKE

The Asia Society, Inc.

Distributed by New York Graphic Society Ltd.

732

FRONTISPIECE: 4 a, b. Wheel of the Doctrine with Crouching Deer.
Dvāravatī style, 7th–9th century. Stone; Wheel, diam. 37¹³⁄₁₆ in.;
Deer, H. 10¼ in. See page 35.
Photographed before the National Museum, Bangkok.

The Sculpture of Thailand is the catalogue of an exhibition shown
in the Asia House Gallery in the fall of 1972 as an activity
of The Asia Society, to further greater understanding between
the United States and the peoples of Asia.

AN ASIA HOUSE GALLERY PUBLICATION.

© *The Asia Society* 1972
Library of Congress Catalogue Card Number 78–186666
SBN: 0–87848–039–0

This project is supported by a grant from the National Endowment
for the Arts in Washington, D.C., a Federal agency.
The unusual quality of the catalogue has been made possible by a
grant from the Ford Motor Company Fund.

Contents

Acknowledgments

The exhibition of Thai sculpture for which this catalogue has been prepared was originally suggested to us by Ambassador Kenneth T. Young, then President of The Asia Society. He felt that sufficient new material had been discovered within the past decade to make possible another fine exhibition without using any of the works of art which had been included in *The Arts of Thailand* of 1960–62. Such encouragement from the former Ambassador from the United States to Thailand was strongly supported by other advisers. These included Miss Elizabeth Lyons of the University Museum of The University of Pennsylvania, who had recently assisted with the new installations of the National Museum of Thailand; Professor Theodore Bowie of Indiana University, who had helped organize the earlier exhibition; and the distinguished scholar Mr. Alexander B. Griswold. But it was not until we received the generous assurances of the Minister of Foreign Affairs of Thailand, His Excellency Mr. Thanat Khoman, and those of the Minister of Education and Culture, His Excellency Mr. Sukich Nimmanaheminda, that we could begin work on this auspicious project.

Now, as the exhibition is finally realized, we rejoice that His Majesty King Bhūmibol Adulyadej and Her Majesty Queen Sirikit of Thailand have agreed to act as its patrons. Their royal condescension both as patrons and as private lenders will be deeply appreciated by all American admirers of the people and arts of Thailand.

Since the beginning of our undertaking, encouragement was given by His Excellency Mr. Sunthorn Hongladarom, the Ambassador of Thailand in Washington, and by Mr. Chua Sariman, Director General of Fine Arts. Among kind officials in Thailand who were soon to aid us were Mr. Bunthin Attagora, Under-Secretary of State for Education, Mr. Noom Yoonaidharma, Deputy Director of Fine Arts, Mr. Somporn Yupho, and Mrs. Chira Chongkol, Mr. Nikom Musigakama, and Mr. Kamthornthep Krataithong of the Bangkok National Museum.

During the summer of 1970, Professor Bowie, having been invited to be the organizer of the exhibition, traveled in Thailand on our behalf. He was accompanied on this trip by Prince Subhadradis Diskul, the eminent Thai scholar and Dean of the Faculty of Archaeology, Silpakorn University, who had agreed to write the descriptive entries for the catalogue. Professor Bowie also conferred with Mr. Alexander B. Griswold, who would later provide one of the learned introductory texts that are here printed.

I, too, journeyed to Thailand in the autumn of that same year to conclude our official agreements and to make final requests for the treasures that The Asia Society hoped to borrow. The Honorable Leonard Unger, United States Ambassador to Thailand, and Mr. Kenneth T. MacCormac, our Cultural Affairs Officer, were both immensely helpful at this juncture, as was Mr. Charles Sheffield, Curator of the James Thompson house, the "House on the Klong," who has generously lent us rare material from Mr. Thompson's collection.

Now, more recently, the difficulties of financing so ambitious an undertaking have been alleviated by a generous grant from the National Endowment for the Arts. Moreover, the unusual quality of the catalogue has been made possible by a grant from the Ford Motor Company Fund.

As a result of all this invaluable assistance, the Asia House Gallery is able to present an up-to-date survey of ancient Siamese art in its various aspects as religious sculpture. Moreover, a new generation will visit this rich and illuminating assemblage of Thai imagery who could not have taken advantage of the exhibition presented a decade earlier.

Let us hope that this special opportunity to view her great sculptural heritage will draw many travelers to Thailand who will discover that even so fine an exhibition as this can only offer a taste of the larger feast.

GORDON B. WASHBURN
Director, Asia House Gallery

Lenders to the Exhibition

His Majesty King Bhūmibol Adulyadej of Thailand

Prince Piyarangsit, Bangkok

Dr. Viroj Kanasut, Bangkok

James H. W. Thompson Collection, Bangkok

National Museum, Ayudhyā

National Museum, Bangkok

National Museum, Chainât (Jayanāda)

National Museum, Gampèng Pet

National Museum, Lampûn

National Museum, Sukhodaya

National Museum, Û Tòng

Foreword

The present exhibition might be termed a direct descendent of "The Arts of Thailand," a large exhibition which was circulated in the United States in 1960–62, then seen in Japan and, after a pause in Bangkok where it was also placed on view, continued on to various countries in Western Europe. This Asia Society presentation, however, as the title of the exhibition reveals, is confined to one expression of the art of Thailand, namely its sculpture. Such an assemblage of fine and rare pieces, including so large a number of early examples, has not been seen previously in the United States.

Many of those responsible for the earlier event have participated in this later one. My own functions were identical: head of the selection committee and editor of the catalogue. Both Prince Subhadradis Diskul and Mr. Alexander B. Griswold performed again, the former as principal advisor for the selections and the latter as contributor of texts for the catalogue. The selection committee also included Miss Elizabeth Lyons, whose knowledge of public and private collections in Thailand is unparalleled, and Mr. Gordon B. Washburn, who made all the final decisions.

Special recognition must be made of the extremely cordial cooperation accorded to the project on the part of the Thai Government and its representatives. Mr. Washburn has already expressed our gratitude to many Thai officials, but in addition we should like to thank particularly those members of the staffs of the Bangkok, Ayudhyā, Û Tòng, Sukhodaya, and Lampûn National Museums, who went out of their way to assist us.

It is a matter of great personal satisfaction for me to have been able to count on the unstinted help of two such outstanding authorities as Prince Diskul and Alexander Griswold, whose contributions to the catalogue are a guarantee of its distinction. Thanks are also owed to Professor Jean Boisselier for numerous valuable suggestions.

I am also grateful for the privilege of using the resources of the Breezewood Foundation at Monkton, Maryland, and for the generous assistance given at all times by its Secretary, Mrs. Mildred Dreher. I also wish to acknowledge the support afforded me by the Faculty Research Committee of Indiana University in the preparation of this catalogue.

First and last, however, I must express my most sincere appreciation for the constant encouragement given me by The Asia Society in the person of the Director of its Gallery, Gordon B. Washburn, and its Assistant Director, Miss Virginia Field. They have been warm and understanding friends.

THEODORE BOWIE
Department of Fine Arts, Indiana University

Introduction

A visitor who comes upon the ancient art of Siam for the first time may quite understandably be baffled by its astonishing variety. Unlike Javanese and Khmer art, where a certain uniformity of style prevails, the sculptures created in the land today known as Thailand have a strongly eclectic look. They reflect numerous influences and crosscurrents in a way that permits them to be labeled as "international," in the same sense that twelfth century Gothic art, early Renaissance painting or contemporary architecture may be described as international, i.e. hybrid. The parallel is indeed a useful one, since Siam, like France or Northwestern India for example, has been historically (and mainly by dint of geographical determinism) a crossroad, a battlefield, and a melting pot.

The present day Kingdom of Thailand is the heir of a succession of states with capitals located in widely different places, where, by turns, the various peoples—Malaysian, Cambodian, Burmese, Tai, Chinese and others—which now constitute the nation originally held sway and claimed hegemony over the other parts. This historical process began about the first century A.D. when a large part of the vast territory which we think of as Southeast Asia was loosely organized into an Indianizing kingdom known to the Chinese as Fu-nan. The culture of the ruling class was therefore largely Indian, and its religion either Brahmanism or Buddhism.

In the states that succeeded Fu-nan, art was predominantly a religious function; basic iconographic themes and cult imagery, imported from India, became transformed first by local conventions and habits and later by the phenomenon of cross-fertilization. Travel—motivated by missionary zeal, the urge for pilgrimage to sacred shrines, trade, and conquest—contributed to the richness of the art found there.

The process is far from having been always peaceful; some destructive aspects are, unhappily, all too visible today. Curiously enough, by comparison with its neighbors Thailand has had a rather fortunate history. It can with some justification claim that it has been an independent nation for a very long time, and that it was never colonized by a European state.

Though not free from its share of political, social, and economic complaints, Thailand gives the impression of being a reasonably prosperous land inhabited by a gentle and easy-going people. This impression is not altogether misleading because for fourteen hundred years the land, whatever its political configurations may have been, has been largely under the sway of Theravāda Buddhism. The term is often translated as meaning the "Doctrine of the Elders," and might perhaps be equated with a modified type of fundamental Buddhism

Ruins at Sukhodaya.

in which the Buddha is primarily venerated as a Teacher. Various influences, including the worship of Hinduistic divinities, have helped to transform the Enlightened One into a compassionate Lord of the Universe. He is, therefore, not only Guide but Savior, and his images have acquired the sacrosanct character of icons. The representation (most often in sculpture) of the Godhead implies that he is the embodiment of all that is good and beautiful.

The esthetic canon involved is a very simple one: an image is beautiful because it is the Buddha, and one image is not more beautiful than any other. Differences in style, by which we Westerners set so much store, must be almost meaningless to the true believer. According to his means he is likely to acquire (perhaps having commissioned them) a number of Buddha images in a variety of postures and of styles and to place them in his home in a place of honor. These have a function equivalent to that of tutelary divinities—or probably a more important one, since a special kind of respect is accorded them. Thais residing in foreign lands have been observed (usually in museums) reverently bowing before Buddha images; they are normally too well bred to express shock when they come upon one used as a casual ornament in an American living room.

Belief in the teachings of the Buddha and the imitation of his moderate and selfless ways have undoubtedly gentled the Thais. Their artists have endeavored, often with signal success, to express in harmonious terms a transcendental Being whose message is one of moderation in all things, infinite mercy, and universal love.

THEODORE BOWIE

Images of the Buddha

By A. B. Griswold

The sculpture of Siam is dominated by images of the Buddha.[1] For more than thirteen centuries the prevailing religion has been Buddhism, usually the Theravāda or "Doctrine of the Elders," sometimes the Mahāyāna or "Greater Vehicle," and images of the Buddha have been made in incalculable numbers.

Every one of them is a copy of an older one, tracing back, in theory, to certain miraculous originals made in India or Ceylon. The copy, however, does not have to *look* like the model; it has to *be* like it. As with successive editions of a book with the same text, the format may change.

As this art is very little understood in the West, it may be helpful to say something about its practice and its conventions.

ANATOMY

Unlike images of Hindu gods, which may have a multiplication of heads and limbs, an image of the Buddha never has more than one head, two arms and two legs.

The Pali Commentarial literature of medieval Ceylon lists thirty-two major "marks" and eighty minor ones which are supposed to have characterized the Buddha's Person.[2] Taken together, they constitute what Coomaraswamy aptly calls the "supernatural anatomy." Every image of the Buddha is thought of as having *all* of these marks even though not all of them are visible to the human eye (and in fact some of those on the list, such as a "sweet and resonant voice," cannot possibly be). In practice a small selection of them is deemed sufficient. In Siam nearly all images of the Buddha are gilded, or once were, to show that his skin was "the color of gold," they have an ushnisha or protuberance of the skull, generally with a finial on top simulating a light-reflecting "jewel" or a flame, the hair is shown in short curls, and the ear lobes are distended. Among the other marks which are sometimes evident are an *ūrṇā* or circle of hair on the forehead, very long arms, fingers of equal length, equal toes, flat footsoles, projecting heels, and an auspicious network of lines on sole and palm.

These are ancient marks of diverse origin. Some are plastic renderings of metaphors; some are Yogic; some are marks that were considered auspicious by the soothsayers who examined a person's whole body much as a palmist examines the hand. At least one is a touch of realism: the Buddha before becoming a monk was a prince who wore the heavy earrings of his time, and after he removed them the ear lobes remained distended. Legend asserts that when he embraced the ascetic life he slashed off his long hair with one blow of his sword, leaving its remains in short individual curls. The long arms recall Yogic exercises of arm-stretching. The Buddha's Person was suffused with "fiery energy" (*teja*), which explains the gold-colored skin, the finial on the ushnisha, and the aureole.

Now and then other features are seen, which are based not on the Pali Commentaries but on stereotyped descriptions of gods and heroes in Sanskrit poetry or (what amounts to the same thing) comparisons with familiar objects prescribed in Indian art manuals as guides to anatomical form, such as a head shaped "like an egg," eyebrows "like drawn bows," nose "like a parrot's beak," chin "like a mango stone," and so on.

53. Footprint of the Buddha. *Sukhodaya style, 14th century. Bronze;* L. 61 ⅞ *in. See page 94.*

POSTURE

An image in the round may be copied from one in bas-relief, or vice versa.

Many bas-reliefs are illustrations of specific incidents in the Buddha's career, with his posture suggesting the action he is performing, while the scenery and the *dramatis personae* help further to identify the incident. When such a figure of the Buddha is copied in the round, if the scenery and the *dramatis personae* are omitted, the identification of the incident may become less certain.

On the other hand instead of portraying an incident in his career, some bas-reliefs portray the place where it occurred, including the temple and commemorative statue erected there by the piety of later generations. In that case the main figure is not so much a representation of the Buddha himself as a copy of the statue, while the auxiliary figures are not persons who were present at the incident but worshipers doing homage to the statue long after the Buddha's death. The posture of the statue might give a clue to the incident, and so might that of a copy in the round, but not necessarily a positive identification.

In the sculpture of Siam there is little evidence of insistence on the exact depiction of the performance of a *mudrā*. In the Theravāda a good deal of freedom is allowed in the iconography of posture, though of course it has to be appropriate to the action the Buddha is performing. Certain postures naturally become associated with certain incidents, but others may occur in the same context, and one posture may serve for more than one incident.

Sculpture portrays the Buddha standing or walking, seated or reclining; sometimes he sits in "western" fashion, but more often with legs crossed (No. 64) or folded one over the other (Nos. 59, 60, etc.). It is very doubtful if the hand-postures of standing or walking images of the Buddha in Siam have the same meanings as in Indian art. There is less uncertainty about the seated images: in the posture of "meditation," for example, both hands are in the lap, while in the Victory over Māra the right hand has moved to the knee, very much as in India. The reclining posture signifies the *parinibbāna* (see No. 48).

THE MONASTIC DRESS

The Buddha is normally shown wearing the "Three Garments" (*ticīvara*) of the monastic dress, or at least two of them. Each is an untailored rectangular piece of cloth.

The undercloth. The first is the undercloth (*antaravāsaka*), which nowadays measures about 3 m. by 1 m. It is worn around the waist like a sarong, with the long axis horizontal, secured by a knot in front, or else held in place by a cloth belt over which the edge of the garment may be turned downward. The garment reaches from the waist almost to the ankles. As 3 m. is more than enough to encircle the waist, the surplus cloth is folded accordion-wise into a "frontal panel," which is allowed to hang down between the legs or is tucked in at one side (Fig. 1, a–d).

The robe. The second garment is the robe (*uttarāsaṅga*), which at present measures about 2 m. by 3 m. It is worn in the same manner as the Greek himation or the Roman pallium. A monk sometimes wears it in the "covering" mode, draped around both shoulders (Fig. 2, a–d), sometimes in the "open" mode, leaving the right shoulder and arm bare (Fig. 2f); in either case it reaches down to the level of the calves, covering the whole of the undercloth except the bottom hem. According to the *Vinaya* or Book of Monastic Discipline, monks must have both shoulders covered when entering a village or town, but should expose the right shoulder when saluting a superior. In practice this means, in present-day Siam, that

A, B

C, D

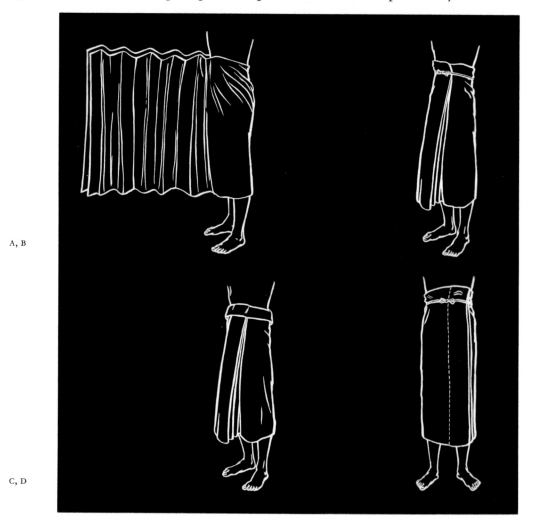

Fig. 1. *The Undercloth*

A. *Composition of the panel.*   B. *Frontal panel, with belt.*
C. *Frontal panel, with overhang covering belt.*   D. *Lateral panel, turned inward.*

Drawings after illustrations in "Imported Images and the Nature of Copying in the Art of Siam," in *Essays offered to G. H. Luce . . . , 2* vols. (Ascona, 1966), ed. Ba Shin, Jean Boisselier, and A. B. Griswold.

when a monk is outdoors in a village or town he wears the robe in the covering mode; when he is in his monastery, he wears it in the open mode; at other times, for example when making a pilgrimage or living in a forest, he wears it in whichever of the two modes may be more convenient.

Apart from the "mode," the robe is subject to an indefinite number of lesser variations or "inflections." As the *Vinaya* takes no cognizance of them we might be inclined to dismiss them as trivialities, but they may be instructive. In the past different sects, and sometimes individual monasteries, established their own rules about the proper inflections to be used on various occasions, and details of this sort were taken so seriously that they sometimes aroused bitter controversy.

In ancient India, as we know from sculpture, when monks were standing or walking they grasped one or more corners of the robe in the left hand to keep it from slipping, but wound them around their left wrist when they sat down. Later on, in Siam, they wound the corners around the wrist when they were standing as well as when seated. Some sects adopted other devices to secure the robe. The one in general use in Siam today is the *lûk buap* or "gourd-roll" inflection, a relatively modern invention that need not concern us here. We shall discuss only those inflections that commonly occur in the sculpture of Siam.

The robe in the covering mode. The monk begins by standing in the "preparatory" position, with the robe passing behind his back and one of the upper corners grasped firmly in his left hand, while part of the upper hem, about 1 m. from the other corner, is held in the fingers of his right hand (Fig. 2a). Then, using his right hand, he drapes the garment counterclockwise around himself, with the upper hem forming the neckline, and throws the free corner backward over his left shoulder (Fig. 2d).

If he drops his hands, the cloth will cover them, and the bottom hem of the robe will make a horizontal circuit of the legs. As both vertical hems are at the left side, he can free his left hand by thrusting it out between them, continuing to hold one corner of the robe in this hand or winding it around the wrist (Fig. 2b).

The usual way for him to free his right hand, as there is no opening at that side, is by means of the "circumflex inflection," raising the bottom hem and thrusting his hand out from under it (Fig. 2c). The bottom hem, beginning behind the left calf, rises in the rear to the right wrist, then falls in front to the left shin where it terminates in a corner of the robe.

If he picks up this corner and adds it to the corner already in his left hand or wound around his wrist, there will be a "U-inflection," in other words the bottom hem will describe a large U running from wrist to wrist (Fig. 2e).

In Siam the great majority of images of the standing Buddha wear the covering mode (there is only one exception in our exhibition, No. 76). Those of the Dvāravatī period (e.g. Nos. 5, 20, 25) nearly always have the U-inflection, which we conclude was part of the monastic practice of the predominant sect. The U-inflection occurs in other schools too (e.g. No. 40), but less regularly.

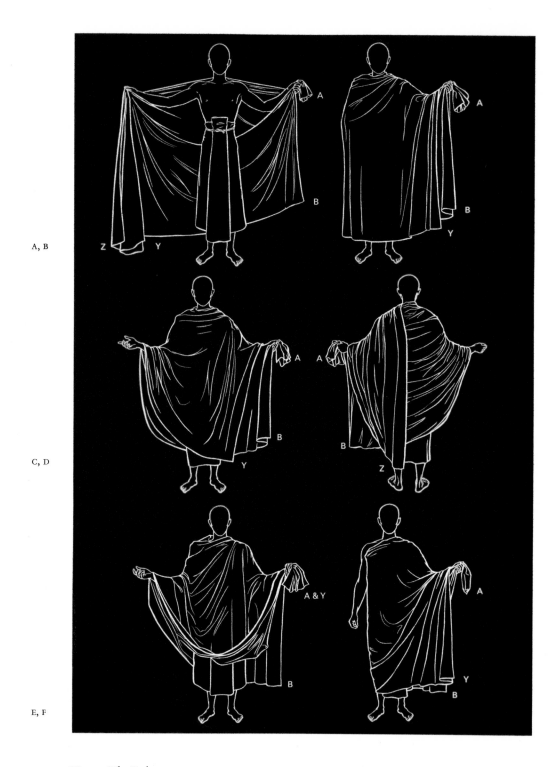

A, B

C, D

E, F

Fig. 2. *The Robe*

A. *Preparatory position.*   B. *The covering mode.*   C. *The covering mode with circumflex inflection.*
D. *The covering mode with circumflex inflection, rear view.*   E. *The U-inflection.*   F. *The open mode.*

18

Fig. 3 *Robe and Shawl.*
The robe is in the open mode with "reversing inflection" and shoulder-flap; the folded shawl is laid on top of the shoulder-flap. In the drawing, for the sake of clarity, the size of the shoulder-flap has been increased and that of the shawl reduced. After Griswold, *Dated Buddha Images of Northern Siam, Artibus Asiae*, Suppl. 16 (1957), p. 74.

The robe in the open mode. The monk, again beginning with the "preparatory" position (Fig. 2a) with one of the upper corners held firmly in his left hand, drapes the robe counter-clockwise around his body, passing it under the right armpit, and throws the free corner over the left shoulder (Fig. 2f). Everything is the same as in the uninflected covering mode (Fig. 2b) except that the right shoulder and arm are bare, and the upper hem, instead of passing around the neck, passes diagonally across the back and the chest.

The open mode is usually accompanied by the "reversing" inflection: the monk, in throwing the corner in his right hand over his left shoulder, thrusts it in *underneath* the cloth that is already there, which he then pulls downward on the chest. Part of this cloth is folded accordion-wise to form a "shoulder-flap" (Nos. 16, 30). The shoulder-flap usually reaches down almost to the waist in front, but sometimes it stops above the nipple; the difference may be sectarian.

Seated images are far more numerous in Siam than those in any other posture. The majority wear the open mode with reversing inflection and shoulder-flap (there are only a few exceptions in our exhibition, e.g. No. 15, which shows the uninflected open mode). Walking and reclining images are comparatively few in number. In Siam they nearly all wear the open mode.

The shawl. The shawl (*saṅghāṭi*) is a duplicate of the robe, originally worn as a cloak over the robe in cool weather. In Siam it is often omitted, but is required for certain occasions. It is then folded accordion-wise in its entirety, and laid over the shoulder-flap of the robe, which is worn in the open mode with reversing inflection (Fig. 3). In sculpture it is often difficult to know whether the strip of cloth seen over the left shoulder is intended to be the shoulder-flap of the robe or the folded shawl on top of it, though sometimes (e.g. No. 64) the distinction is made clear.

THE ROYAL ATTIRE AND THE BUDDHA IMAGE

The Royal Attire of Hindu divinities includes a dhoti (waist-cloth), a diadem, and a profusion of jewelry such as earrings, necklace, armlets, bracelets, finger rings, and anklets. In accordance with a custom originating in India, and amply attested in Khmer epigraphy, the pious might present the statue of a Hindu god with real ornaments of this sort, which could be changed at will.

When Buddhists adopted the practice, they extended it to images which were already wearing the monastic dress. The "Emerald" Buddha in Bangkok, for example, has three changes of raiment in addition to the monastic dress which is an integral part of the statue. In the rainy season he wears a golden wig with the traditional curls, ushnisha-cover, and finial, plus a golden costume simulating a monastic robe in the open mode; in the cool season, he wears the same wig, and a simulated robe in the covering mode; in the hot season the wig is replaced by a royal crown, and the simulated monastic robe by a full set of jewels.

When an image which receives honors of this sort is copied, the aspect of the copy will obviously vary according to the season in which it is made. There is a further complication too: in the copy, some of the ornaments may be reproduced as integral parts of the image, while others may be omitted with the idea of adding real ones later. This may account for peculiarities in some of the images in our exhibition. No. 47, for instance, wears the ordinary monastic dress, an ornamental ushnisha-cover, and no other jewels; No. 45 is similar, but has a decorated brow-band as well; No. 33 shows the hems of the monastic robe where they cross the body and limbs, but the part of the robe that should fall from the left shoulder and arm has been eliminated, as if to facilitate the addition of real ornaments though the image already wears a complete parure of simulated ones; No. 41 seems to be complete in itself, with an orthodox monastic robe, plus diadem, ushnisha-cover, earrings, necklace, and arm-lets; No. 54 wears no diadem or other ornaments except a richly decorated belt and frontal panel, evidently attached to the undercloth and seen through the transparency of the robe.

SCULPTURAL CONVENTIONS

It is easy to be confused by certain conventions used by image-makers.

In standing images, the robe, worn in the covering mode, is generally given the appearance of symmetry at the left and right, especially when both hands are in the same posture. The origin of this convention is obscure. The appearance is purely conventional, for the real robe is always asymmetrically arranged, with all four corners at the left (Figs. 2b, c, d). To achieve the effect of symmetry without taking arbitrary liberties with the arrangement of

48. Reclining Buddha. "*Û Tòng A*" *or* "*B*" *style*, 13*th–*14*th century. Bronze;* L. 15⅜ *in.*
See page 88. Photographed at the temple of the Great Relic, Ayudhyā.

the garment requires some ingenuity. The difficulty is increased by the habitual circumflex inflection, which leaves two corners of the robe dangling near the left leg, but makes the bottom hem describe two large curves at the corresponding position at the right, one behind and one in front (Figs. 2c, d). The U-inflection removes one of the corners and makes the front of the robe symmetrical, but it does nothing for the other corner and the back of the robe. The obvious solution is either to square off the curve at the right or to round off the corner at the left.

In No. 20 the first method is adopted. In order to provide a plausible explanation, the robe is draped loosely enough in the rear to release the tension that makes the hem curve upward at the right, and let it droop to the same level as the corner at the left, while the cloth falling from the outer side of both wrists is gathered into a few pleats whose zigzag ends can be seen at the bottom of the robe, each group balancing the other. In No. 71 a compromise method is adopted, with the corner at the right partly rounded and the curve at the left partly squared, so that both sides are brought into apparent conformity.

The real monastic dress is made of opaque cloth; but in accordance with a convention that began in Gupta India the dress of nearly all images of the Buddha in Siam appears thin and clinging. That is because the radiance of his Person, diffused by his "fiery energy," is thought of as shining through the cloth, making it transparent, so that the garments are reduced to a silhouette where they fall free, and a pattern of hems where they lie on the body or limbs.

The transparency of the dress may give the impression that the Buddha's torso is nude; but if there is a reserve of cloth between the body and the left arm, we can be sure he is wearing the robe in the open mode; and if there is a reserve of cloth between the body and both arms, the robe is in the covering mode.

When a monk is standing up, the only visible part of his undercloth is the small section that hangs below the bottom of the robe. In standing images (e.g. No. 54) this part is usually visible too, while in seated ones it is shown as a hem crossing each ankle (e.g. Nos. 29, 59, 60, 80). In addition the transparency of the robe may allow the upper edge of the undercloth to be seen at the waist (e.g. Nos. 5, 20, 42). To the untrained eye it may look as if the undercloth were worn outside the robe, which is of course impossible, but as soon as the convention is understood the arrangement is seen to be logical. When critics accuse an image-maker of misunderstanding the monastic dress it is generally because they themselves misunderstand the convention. Some sculptors made mistakes, but more often from carelessness or incompetence than misunderstanding. It is hard to believe that any of them did not know what the real monastic dress was like.

The convention of transparency requires other departures from visual reality. When a monk wearing the robe in the covering mode is standing up, the garment has a distinct rotundity; indeed if he holds both hands in front of his shoulders, the lower half of the robe, thought of schematically, is almost cylindrical. In sculpture, however, it looks more like a flattish envelope enclosing the legs. In No. 20, if we disregard the clumsy repairs at the ankles, the part of the robe behind the legs is approximately a rectangle, on which the U-shaped front of the robe is loosely inscribed. In reality the front of the robe would fall vertically from the wrists, but in order to allow it to "cling" to the abdomen and legs, and thus reveal their contours intelligibly, the sculptor has pushed it backward until it looks as if it were glued to the rectangular plane behind it. He has sacrificed the rotundity of the garment to make the radiance of the Buddha's Person manifest.

The *Vinaya* requires monks to wear the robe in a neat and seemly manner, with the lower edge as nearly horizontal as the inflections will allow. In No. 20, however, the bottom hem hangs much lower behind the legs than in front where it describes the U. This difference in level, which would be needlessly untidy and in contravention of the disciplinary rules, is not to be taken literally. It is simply a matter of "anamorphosis," a convention employed in the Indianizing world by which the artist may shift our point of view in relation to one particular detail, so as to allow us to see it clearly.

In Nos. 40 and 54 the curvature of the bottom hem of the robe behind the legs should not be taken literally either, for if it were really lower in the middle than at the sides it too would be in violation of the *Vinaya* rule. If we imagine this curvature transposed into the horizontal plane, we shall recognize a case of anamorphosis intended to restore a sense of rotundity to the robe without dimming the Buddha's radiance.

In seated images, if there is no anamorphosis, the shoulder-flap is shown lying flat on the chest and ending squarely (Nos. 41, 49), so that the pleats composing it are invisible, just as they would be in reality. Often however the tip of the shoulder-flap is shown in anamorphosis, as if it were slanted slightly upward so as to reveal the pleat-ends, which are then rendered in the form of a notched fish-tail (Nos. 59, 60). Sometimes the anamorphosis extends farther, as if the pleats were turned a little sidewise, or beginning to come open, so as to allow us to see more of them (Nos. 19, 30).

Another sort of anamorphosis reduces the size of a piece of cloth to let us see the cloth under it, which in reality would be hidden. When there is a folded shawl (*saṅghāṭi*) over the shoulder, it is usually the same size as the shoulder-flap of the robe, and so hides it; but in No. 60, in order to let us see both, the shawl is made a little narrower and shorter; and in order to distinguish them clearly from each other, the shawl is made to end squarely, while the shoulder-flap below it ends in a notched fish-tail.

Once we start looking for anamorphosis we can find it much more often than we suspected. In No. 56, for example, the Buddha appears to be facing forward but walking sidewise in the doorway of a temple—certainly an odd thing to do if taken literally—but we have no difficulty in recognizing the posture of the feet as a piece of anamorphosis which defines the walking posture. It seems more probable, indeed, that the figure does not represent the Buddha himself, but a great cult statue of him; and as such statues are not usually placed in doorways we can take it for granted that this one is supposed to be in the center

of the temple, and seen through the temple doorway. Furthermore when vases of flowers are presented to a statue by the faithful, they are normally put in front of the statue, not outside the temple; but this pair is so large that if they were shown in their normal place they would hide half the statue. They have therefore been transposed by anamorphosis to either side, just as the statue has been transposed forward.

A far more drastic type of anamorphosis occurs in three images in our exhibition, Nos. 29, 30, and 42. In the sixth week after his Enlightenment, according to the texts, the Buddha was seated in deep meditation beside a pond, when a torrential rainstorm came up and the flood-waters began to rise. A Nāgarāja (Serpent King), seeing that the Buddha was in danger but not wishing to disturb his meditation, spread his seven-headed hood above him to shelter him from the rain, and at the same time, in order to protect him from the rising water, coiled his body *around* him: on the last point the texts are specific. Occasionally, indeed, nineteenth-century Siamese painting portrays the incident with only the Buddha's head visible and his body completely hidden by the Nāga's coils; but sculpture, rejecting such eccentric literalism, invariably represents the subject in anamorphosis, removing the figure of the Buddha to a place of safety where he can be clearly seen, seated on top of the coiled body of the Nāga.

NOTES

1. The reader may wonder why I persist in using the name *Siam*, since the country is today officially called *Thailand*. The latter is a translation of *Müang Tai* (or *Thai*, as it is often written, though in any case pronounced nearly like the English word "tie"). I am writing about the past, and to a considerable extent about the country before the Tai were settled there: to call it "the land of the Tai" would be needlessly confusing. Though the name *Siam* is admittedly an anachronism for the early period, long usage authorizes it as a purely geographical expression. As to *Tai* and *Siamese*, which are more or less interchangeable, it is sometimes convenient to make a distinction, using *Tai* for members of that race whatever country they were living in, and *Siamese* for citizens of Siam, no matter what their racial origin. (From *The Arts of Thailand* [Bloomington, 1960], p. 17).

2. The traditional date of the Buddha's death is 544 B.C., though modern scholarship is inclined to put it some eighty years later. After his death his teachings, as remembered by his disciples, were passed on to large numbers of other monks who were assigned the duty of memorizing them systematically. It was not until the first century B.C. that his teachings began to be put down in writing. Though the work was done in Ceylon, the language used was Pali, a North Indian dialect which orthodox Theravādins believe was used by the Buddha himself. Pali is the sacred language of Theravāda Buddhism, and the Pali Canon is its final authority. In addition an enormous mass of non-Canonical Pali literature has grown up, consisting of Commentaries on the Canon and Commentaries on the Commentaries, composed by learned monks over a long period of time, chiefly in Ceylon but to some extent in other Theravādin countries.

Chronology

DVĀRAVATĪ STYLE	6th–11th century
ŚRĪVIJAYA STYLE	8th–13th century
LOPBURÎ STYLE	11th–14th century
SUKHODAYA STYLE	13th–15th century
Û TÒNG STYLE	13th–15th century
STYLES OF NORTHERN THAILAND	14th–20th century
AYUDHYĀ STYLE	15th to late 18th century
BANGKOK STYLE	Late 18th century to present

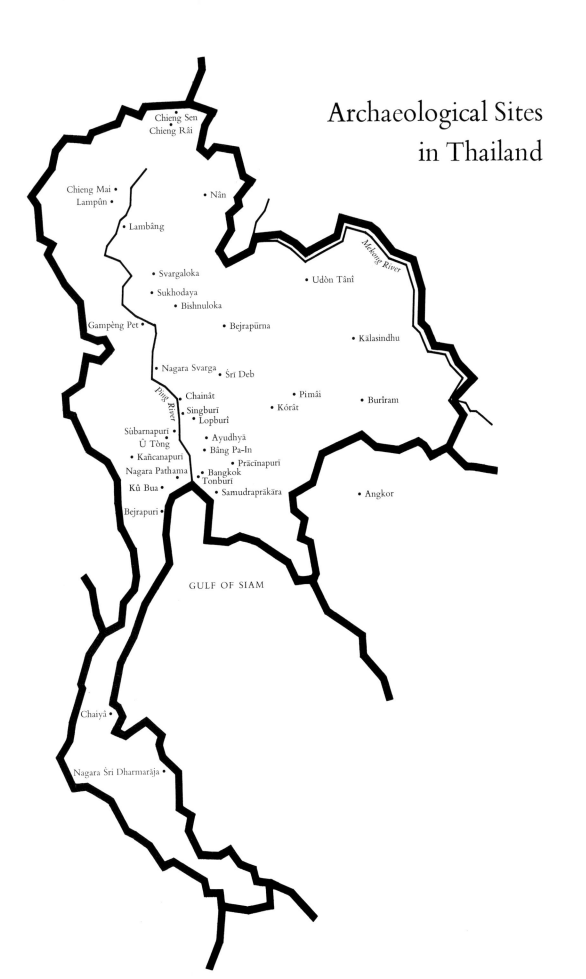

Archaeological Sites
in Thailand

Chieng Sen •
Chieng Râi •

Chieng Mai •
Lampûn •

• Nân

Mekong River

• Lambâng

• Svargaloka

• Sukhodaya

• Bishnuloka

• Udòn Tânî

• Bejrapūrna

Gampèng Pet •

• Kālasindhu

• Nagara Svarga

• Śrī Deb

Ping River

• Chainât

• Pimâi

• Kórât

• Burîram

• Singburī

• Lopburî

Súbarnapurī •

• Ayudhyā

Û Tòng •

• Bâng Pa-In

• Kañcanapuri

• Prācīnapurī

Nagara Pathama •

• Bangkok

Tonburī •

Kû Bua •

• Samudraprākāra

• Angkor

Bejrapuri •

GULF OF SIAM

Chaiyâ •

Nagara Śri Dharmarāja •

27

(*Above*) 7 a, b. Two Bas-reliefs in Repoussé. *Dvāravatī style, 7th–9th century. Gold; a.* H. 2¹¹⁄₁₆ *in., b.* H. 2¹⁄₁₆ *in.*
See page 37.

(*Below*) 66 a, b, c. Three Votive Plaques. a, b. *"Û Tòng C" style, early 15th century. c. Ayudhyā style, 15th–16th
century. Gold repoussé;* H. 2³⁄₈ *in. to 3¹⁄₁₆ in. See page 112.*

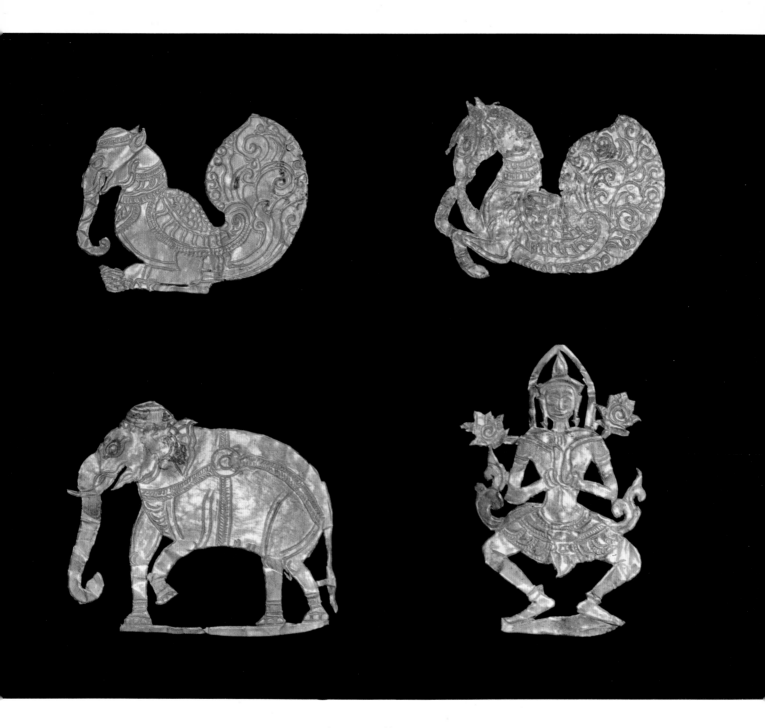

67 a, b, c, d. Four Votive Plaques. *Ayudhyā style, 15th–16th century. Gold repoussé;* H. 2 9/16 *in. to 4 ⅛ in. See page* 112.

30

Catalogue

By M. C. Subhadradis Diskul

1   The Bodhisattva Avalokiteśvara

Śrīvijaya style, 7th–8th century
Stone; H. 45¼ in. (115 cm.)
National Museum, Bangkok

This statue, discovered at Chaiyâ in Peninsular Thailand, is one of the earliest and most beautiful stone sculptures of the Śrīvijaya school. The hair style reminds us of the Indian Gupta and Post-Gupta schools. A broken figurine of the Buddha Amitābha in the lower part of the chignon identifies the figure as Avalokiteśvara, and the antelope skin can be seen hanging from the left shoulder. This slender, smiling Bodhisattva wears a long dhoti secured by a narrow cloth belt. Broken portions of stone projecting from the legs may be the remains of the Bodhisattva's hands or attributes; there are other projecting remnants, of uncertain function.

Publ.: George Coedès, *Les collections archéologiques du Musée National de Bangkok, Ars Asiatica* 12 (Paris, 1928), pl. 12.

2   The Bodhisattva Avalokiteśvara

Dvāravatī style, 7th–8th century (?)
Terra cotta; H. 35¹³⁄₁₆ in. (91 cm.)
National Museum, Bangkok

This beautiful image and its companion piece (No. 3) are justly regarded as equal in quality to the best Dvāravatī work in terra cotta, and superior to the best in stucco. It was discovered in the course of excavating a ruined monument south of the town of Kû Bua, near Râtburî (Rājapurī) in Southern Thailand. The hair style, broad shoulders, and slim body are reminiscent of Indian Gupta and Post-Gupta art. The face has a gentle and smiling expression. The figure wears a long dhoti secured by a cloth belt. The profile of an antelope's head can be discerned on the scarf, and identifies the image as the Bodhisattva Avalokiteśvara whose characteristic garment is an antelope skin. The right hand holds the water-pot, an attribute of Avalokiteśvara. The discovery of this Bodhisattva is important, because it is the first proof to come to light that Mahāyāna Buddhism was practiced in the cultural orbit of Dvāravatī, where the great majority of surviving antiquities are associated with the Theravāda.

3   A Bodhisattva (?)

Dvāravatī style, 7th–8th century (?)
Terra cotta; H. *33½ in. (85 cm.)*
National Museum, Bangkok

The provenance is the same as for No. 2, and the figures are very similar. If, as seems probable, they formed a pair in an architectural composition, it may be concluded that this figure is also a Bodhisattva, but whatever clues to his identity there may once have been are now lost.

4 a,b   Wheel of the Doctrine with Crouching Deer   *(frontispiece)*

Dvāravatī style, 7th–9th century
Stone; a. *Wheel, diam. 37¹³⁄₁₆ in. (96 cm.);* b. *Deer,* H. *10¼ in. (26 cm.)*
National Museum, Bangkok

The Dhammacakka (Wheel of the Doctrine), accompanied by a pair of crouching deer (only one of which is preserved in this example), was an aniconic symbol of the Buddha preaching the First Sermon in the Deer Park near Benares. This Dhammacakka is one of several discovered at Nagara Paṭhama (for this site, see No. 18). Some Thai scholars believe that Nagara Paṭhama was the port of Suvaṇṇabhūmi, the "Land of Gold," to which, according to the Ceylon Chronicles, two Buddhist missionaries were sent by King Asoka the Great of India, who reigned in the third century B.C. It is thought by some that these Wheels go back to that period. Although it is true that such aniconic symbols were in use before the beginning of the Christian Era, when it was not yet the practice to represent the Buddha in human form, there are difficulties with this theory.

First, there is no known tradition or epigraphic evidence to associate Nagara Paṭhama with Suvaṇṇabhūmi, whereas there is a firmly held tradition, set forth in the Kalyāṇī inscription of 1476 A.D. at Pegu in Lower Burma, which identifies the landing-place of the two missionaries with a site near Pegu. Second, the motifs carved on the Wheels discovered in Thailand derive from the Gupta art of India (fourth-sixth century), so the earliest possible date for them would be several hundred years after Asoka's time. It could nevertheless be argued that, even if the missionaries landed somewhere near Pegu, Nagara Paṭhama could have been an important town of the kingdom of Suvaṇṇabhūmi, to which the Doctrine was brought not long afterward, and the absence of a tradition to that effect is not conclusive. It could also be argued that these Wheels could have been carved during the Dvāravatī period in imitation of models, now lost, which were brought by the Asokan missionaries. While a number of aniconic Wheels of the Doctrine have been found at Nagara Paṭhama and elsewhere in Central Thailand, none have been reported from Burma or elsewhere in Southeast Asia.

This Wheel is carved on both faces. It has twenty-two column-like spokes on each. The pedestal has a base carved with lotus petals, then a row of beads, and a triangular composition of leaves (?). These motifs, like those on the Wheel itself, are reminiscent of Gupta art. Like several others, the Wheel has a hole pierced through it above the hub. The purpose of the hole is not known.

5   Standing Buddha

Dvāravatī style, 7th–9th century
Bronze; H. 19 ⁵⁄₁₆ in. (49 cm.)
National Museum, Bangkok

This image, discovered in the crypt of a stupa at Chöng Tâ in Nonburî Province, north of Bangkok, may be ascribed to the early part of the Dvāravatī period. The curls of hair are comparatively large, the ushnisha has no finial, and the facial features resemble those of Indian prototypes rather more than is usual in the Dvāravatī native style. This suggests that the sculptor may have been trained by Indian masters, or at least in a tradition implanted by Indian masters not many generations earlier.

    The Buddha wears the robe in the covering mode with the U-inflection. As with nearly all images of the Buddha in Thailand, the dress appears to be transparent. Both hands are raised, with thumb and forefinger joined, whereas in classical Indian images of the standing Buddha only the right hand performs a gesture, while the left hand grasps one or more corners of the robe to hold it in place. Here, instead, the robe is secured and the U-inflection held in place by folding two corners of the robe together into pleats and winding them around the left wrist; they are then thrown over the forearm, where their pleats may be seen terminating in a zigzag pattern. This no doubt reflects the monastic practice in the community where the image was made.

In Indian iconography the posture of the right hand raised with thumb and forefinger joined is known as *vitarkamudrā*, the "gesture of exposition," but we do not know its significance in Dvāravatī art, whether performed by one or both hands. The attitude of the Buddha portrayed here is now generally regarded in Thailand as signifying the Descent from the Tāvatimsa Heaven. In certain Dvāravatī bas-reliefs this attitude is assumed by the Buddha when he is flanked by the gods Indra and Brahmā, and in Indian iconography the Descent from the Tāvatimsa is one of the incidents in which they accompany him. The main difficulty is that in all scenes that can be definitely identified as the Descent from the Tāvatimsa Heaven the Buddha is portrayed in some other posture.

In Theravāda Legends the Tāvatimsa is the heaven of Indra, on the summit of Meru. It is the second in the ascending scale of the six "heavens of desire."

6   Head from an Image of a Divinity or Dvārapāla (Gate-Guardian)

Dvāravatī style, 7th–9th century
Terra cotta; H. 15 *in.* (38 *cm.*)
National Museum, Bangkok

The head was discovered in the ruins of a monument (designated as number 40) outside the town of Kû Bua. It is an early example of the skill with which the modeler could render a serenely sweet expression in terra cotta. The Western sculptor's practice of creating only a head or a bust is virtually unknown in the Southeast Asian tradition. The multitude of heads or busts of the Buddha or of Hindu divinities which we encounter in museums are the result of accidents or of deliberate mutilation.

7 a,b   Two Bas-reliefs in Repoussé   *(Illustrated p. 28)*

Dvāravatī style, 7th–9th century
Gold; a. H. 2¹¹⁄₁₆ *in.* (6.9 *cm.*); b. H. 2 ¹⁄₁₆ *in.* (5.2 *cm.*)
James H. W. Thompson Collection, Bangkok

a. The Bodhisattva Maitreya, identified by the representation of a stupa in his headdress, sits with legs folded at the ankles, a posture that recalls the art of Amarāvatī. The raised right hand has the fingers bent in what appears to be a variant of the gesture of exposition (*vitarkamudrā*), while the left hand holds a water-pot. In the background, at one side of the Bodhisattva's head, is a stupa (?); at the other, a Wheel of the Doctrine.

b. The Bodhisattva Padmapāṇi holds a lotus in his right hand and an indistinct object in his left. The posture is much the same as in No. 7a.

Publ.: William Warren, *The House on the Klong* (New York, 1968), p. 84, pls. 28, 32.

8   Head from an Image of the Buddha

Dvāravatī style, 8th–9th century
Gold; H. 2¼ *in. (5.3 cm.)*
National Museum, Ū Tòng

Discovered in the ruins of a monument (designated as number 2) at the village of Ū Tòng, this small fragment of a votive image is stylistically half-way between the Gupta prototype and the native Dvāravatī manner.

9   Head from an Image of the Buddha or of a Divinity

Dvāravatī style, 8th–9th century
Terra cotta; H. 5¹⁵⁄₁₆ *in.* (*15 cm.*)
National Museum, Bangkok

This fragment was excavated at Kû Bua near Râtburî (Rājapurī), Southern Thailand. It is very close stylistically to Number 6, but here only the facial features remain.

10 a   Head from a Statue of the Bodhisattva Maitreya

Dvāravatī style, 8th–9th century
Stone; H. 13¹¹⁄₁₆ in. (34.7 cm.)
National Museum, Bangkok (formerly in the James H. W. Thompson Collection)

The head was discovered in a cave near the town of Śrī Deb, province of Petchabûn (Bejrapūrṇa), Northern Thailand. Maitreya, identified by the figure of a stupa in his headdress, is the Bodhisattva who is now waiting in the Tusita Heaven until the time comes, aeons in the future, for him to descend to earth, be reborn as a human being, and achieve Buddhahood to re-create the religion which, according to an old prophecy, is destined to disappear in the year 5000 of the present Buddhist Era (4457 A.D.). The Tusita (Tuśita in Sanskrit) is the fourth in the ascending scale of the six "heavens of desire."

10 b   Head from a Colossal Image of a Bodhisattva

Khmer or Khmerizing style, Pre-Angkorean period, 8th–9th century
Bronze; H. 27⁹⁄₁₆ in. (70 cm.)
National Museum, Bangkok

In Nön Sûng district, in the province of Kórât, in 1961, bulldozing activity led to the discovery of the head and three forearms of what was evidently a four-armed deity, and both legs. It is logical to infer from these fragments, of one of the largest bronzes of this kind ever found, that it was a standing image, with an estimated height of seven feet. Some idea of its appearance may possibly be derived from the small (H. 38 inches) image in the Rockefeller Collection (cf. Sherman E. Lee, *Asian Art: Selections from the Collection of Mr. and Mrs. John D. Rockefeller 3rd* [New York, 1970], pl. 23, where it is identified as "Standing Maitreya").

With regard to the head, Jean Boisselier, who had an opportunity to study it in detail while it was still in the Kórât Museum, speaks with admiration not only of the technical perfection of the lost-wax casting, which is completely free of flaws, but of the "naturalism and handsomeness of the features, the sure modeling, the sense of volume . . . and the exceptional plastic qualities of the mutilated image." One may therefore assume that he was referring to the head before its extensive restoration.

Attention is particularly drawn to the headdress, which is technically called a *jaṭāmukuṭa* (crown of matted hair arranged in the shape of a miter). The irregular, empty space in the front was undoubtedly filled by a symbol (stupa or figure of a meditating Buddha) identifying a particular Bodhisattva—Maitreya or Avalokiteśvara. Boisselier inclines toward the former.

Publ.: Jean Boisselier, "Notes sur l'art du bronze dans l'ancien Cambodge," *Artibus Asiae* 29 (1967): 284–290.

11   The Bodhisattva Avalokiteśvara

Śrīvijaya style, 8th–9th century
Bronze; H. 11¼ in. (28.5 cm.)
Collection of Dr. Viroj Kanasut, Bangkok

This beautiful image, discovered at Prācīṇapurī, not far from Bangkok, stands in the posture of *tribhaṇga* or triple flexion, and has twelve arms. Though some of the attributes held in the hands are indistinct, a lotus, a book (?), a club, and a water-pot can be discerned in the right hands, while one of the left hands performs the gesture of dispelling fear (*abhayamudrā*) and another that of bestowing favors (*varadamudrā*). The Bodhisattva is identified by a figurine of Amitābha in his headdress. The long dhoti is reminiscent of Indian or Javanese costumes.

Publ.: M. C. Subhadradis Diskul, *Masterpieces from Private Collections*, English-Language Series of the Faculty of Archaeology, Silpakorn University, no. 2 (Bangkok, 1970), pp. 8, 9, pl. 15.

12   The Bodhisattva Avalokiteśvara or Padmapāṇi

Śrīvijaya style, 8th–9th century
Bronze; H. 13⅜ in. (34 cm.)
National Museum, Bangkok

The Bodhisattva, identified by a figurine of Amitābha in the headdress, wears a diadem decorated with large floral motifs and a *jaṭāmukuṭa* with locks of hair falling over the shoulders in typical Śrīvijayan style. The ornaments include earrings, necklace, armlets, and bracelets. It is not clear whether or not the scarf is made of antelope skin. A tiger skin is worn over the long dhoti, with the head and forelegs of the animal visible on the right thigh, while the tail and a hind leg are seen on the left. The Bodhisattva's right hand performs the *varadamudrā* (gesture of bestowing favors), while the left hand holds a lotus in accordance with his epithet, Padmapāṇi, "[holding a] lotus in [the] hand." In the back are the remains of a tenon meant to hold an aureole which is now lost.

43

13   Indra or Vajrapāṇi

Dvāravatī style, 8th–9th century
Terra cotta; H. 25 ⁹⁄₁₆ *in.* (64 *cm.*)
National Museum, Bangkok

This terra cotta was discovered in the ruins of the same monument as Nos. 2 and 3. The somewhat inferior quality and the more profuse ornamentation suggest a later date. The object in the left hand is apparently a thunderbolt (*vajra*), the attribute of the god Indra in Theravāda Buddhism and of the Bodhisattva Vajrapāṇi in the Mahāyāna.

14   Standing Buddha

Dvāravatī style, 8th–9th century
Stone; H. 40¹⁵⁄₁₆ *in.* (104 *cm.*)
James H. W. Thompson Collection, Bangkok

This statue was discovered at Lopburî, the site of one of the most important cities of the Dvāravatī period. The curls are large, and there is no finial on the ushnisha. The facial features, while still reminiscent of Indian prototypes, have evolved somewhat more toward the Dvāravatī native type than those of No. 5. The Buddha wears the monastic robe in the covering mode. The missing hands were probably in the same posture as in No. 5. The body is straight, rather than flexed in the *tribhaṅga* attitude as is usual in Dvāravatī art when the left hand is held downward.

Publ.: Warren, *House on the Klong,* p. 85, pl. 41.

15   Buddha Subduing Māra

Dvāravatī style, 8th–9th century
Bronze; H. 10 ¹⁄₁₆ *in. (25.5 cm.)*
National Museum, Bangkok

The Buddha sits with loosely crossed legs, somewhat as in Amarāvatī art. The facial features seem to be transitional between the Indianizing type and those of the Dvāravatī native style. His curls are rather large. The finial on the ushnisha represents a jewel. The base has no decoration whatever, perhaps because it was intended to be set inside a separate outer pedestal covered with lotus petals. The arrangement of the monastic robe, worn in the open mode without reversing inflection or shoulder-flap, suggests a date no later than the ninth century. (See Appendix A, p. 131, for the story of the Buddha subduing Māra.)

16 Buddha Seated in Meditation
Dvāravatī style, 8th–9th century
Stone, lacquered and gilded; H. without tenon, 55⅛ in. (140 cm.); tenon, 17¾ in. (45 cm.)
National Museum, Ayudhyā

The head of this Buddha from Wat Nâng Gui, Ayudhyā, is typical of the school of Dvāravatī, with a large ushnisha, big curls, joined eyebrows, prominent eyes, and thick lips. An aureole and a mandorla are carved in the stele, which has been lacquered in red. The robe is worn in the open mode with reversing inflection and a pleated shoulder-flap, which suggests a date around the middle of the Dvāravatī period. The legs are folded loosely in a manner characteristic of the Indian style of Amarāvatī.

Publ.: Pierre Dupont, *L'archéologie mône de Dvāravatī* (Paris, 1959), pp. 240–245, fig. 478 (wrongly attributed to Chaiyâ); Louis Frédéric, *Sud-est asiatique, ses temples, ses sculptures* (Paris, 1964), fig. 21.

48

17   Mukhaliṅga

     Śrīvijaya style, 8th–9th century
     Stone; H. 42¹⁵⁄₁₆ *in. (109 cm.)*
     National Museum, Bangkok

This phallic emblem of Śiva was discovered at Nòng Wâi in Chaiyâ District, Surāṣṭradhānī Province in Southern Thailand. Most Indian liṅgas are plain, but some are carved with the face of Śiva. The details of the god's face are clear in spite of the damage to which the emblem has been subjected, and the influence of the Gupta style is easily discernible. The expression on the deity's face seems rather stern. His hair is pulled up in a kind of chignon with two parts, each falling backward on top of the head.

Cf. Dupont, *La statuaire préangkorienne, Artibus Asiae*, Suppl. 15 (Ascona, 1955), pl. 21 B and C.

Publ.: S. J. O'Connor, "Note on a *Mukhaliṅga* from Western Borneo," *Artibus Asiae* 29 (1967): 93–98, fig. 4.

18 a,b,c Three Reliefs from the Cūlapadonacetiya

     Dvāravatī style, 8th–9th century
     Stucco; each 47¼ in. sq. (120 cm.)
     National Museum, Û Tòng

Nagara Paṭhama has long been known for the antiquities of Dvāravatī style which have been unearthed there in abundance. The town is dominated by a huge stupa, the Paṭhamacetiya, built in the 1860's on top of a much earlier monument which is completely hidden by it. The Dvāravatī city, 2 km. by 3.7 km. in area, lay a little to the east of the present town. Its approximate center is marked by the Padonacetiya, "monument of the measuring-cup" (an allusion to the cup used to measure out the Buddha's bodily relics to be shared among eight groups of princes).

    Near the Padonacetiya is a monument known as Cūlapadonacetiya, "the lesser Padonacetiya" (the "Wat Pra Patón" of western writers), which was partially excavated in 1939–40 by the late Pierre Dupont and Luang Boribal Buribhand. Further excavations were made there in 1968 by the Department of Fine Arts and Professor Jean Boisselier, chief of the French Archaeological Mission. Their studies showed that the monument was twice rebuilt and enlarged, the new structure in each case covering but not destroying its predecessor.

    The original monument, built in the seventh century, had a series of terra cotta reliefs around the base. In the late eighth or early ninth century the monument was rebuilt; the base was enlarged

18 a

and the terra cottas, by that time much decayed, were covered over. A series of new stucco reliefs was set up around the enlarged base. Most of these appear to represent Jātaka tales (edifying stories of the Buddha's previous lives), though the precise identification is difficult. Others are representations of Bodhisattvas of the Mahāyāna pantheon, whose dress and jewelry seem to have been inspired by the art of Śrīvijaya. At an uncertain date, probably in the late ninth or early tenth century, the monument was again enlarged and the stucco reliefs were covered over. This time no new reliefs were added. In the first and third phase, it appears, the monument was dedicated to the Theravāda, whereas in the second phase the Mahāyāna had at least a share in the honors.

18 b

These three reliefs belong to the second phase, which Professor Boisselier places in the late eighth or early ninth century. They were originally polychromed, and some traces of color can still be seen on them.

The first (No. 18a) shows five seated male figures, plus a fragment of a sixth. They all carried swords in decorated sheaths, only three of which have survived.

The principal figure in the second relief (No. 18b) is a richly attired personage seated in the posture of "royal ease." The remains of an aureole behind his head show that he is a god, and his large belly almost certainly identifies him as Kuvera, the god of wealth. Behind him the heads and shoulders of two attendants remain; each holds a fly-whisk (*cāmara*). The composition is framed in a pair of columns like those of the real architecture of the Dvāravatī period.

The third plaque (No. 18c) is dominated by the figure of a richly attired princess. Beside her are two ladies holding up some sort of offering, while a fat man squats in front of them, holding a fan in his hand. At the other side are two male figures, probably demons; one holds a child, possibly the Bodhisattva who is being abducted by them.

Publ.: Jean Boisselier, "Récentes recherches à Nakhon Pathom," *Journal of the Siam Society* 58 (1970): 55–65.

18 c

19   Buddha Seated in Meditation

Dvāravatī style, 8th–9th century
Terra cotta; H. 17¾ *in.* (45 *cm.*)
National Museum, Û Tòng

The conical finial on the ushnisha indicates a date in the middle of the Dvāravatī period or later, and the facial features are typical of the Dvāravatī native style. The top of the undercloth is seen at the waist, through the "transparency" of the robe. The image was discovered at Û Tòng.

20   Standing Buddha

Dvāravatī style, 8th–9th century
Bronze; H. 16½ *in.* (42 cm.)
National Museum, Bangkok

This bronze, discovered at Udòn Tânî (Uttaradhānī) in Northeastern Thailand, probably belongs to the middle Dvāravatī period. There is no finial on the ushnisha. The facial features are typical of the Dvāravatī native style. The profile of the body is very thin, which is characteristic of the stone statues of the Buddha of the later Dvāravatī period. The posture of the hands is the same as in No. 5.

The robe is worn in the covering mode, with the U-inflection shown in pronounced anamorphosis (see p. 18).

Publ.: Dupont, *L'archéologie mône . . .* , pp. 217, 218. fig. 454; Coedès, *Les collections archéologiques . . .* , *Ars Asiatica* 12, pl. 4.

21   The Bodhisattva Maitreya with Attendants

Śrīvijaya style, 8th–9th century
Bronze; H. 7⅞ in. (20 cm.)
National Museum, Bangkok

The Bodhisattva sits on a high-backed throne with a parasol above and lion supports below. The head is like that of a Buddha, but the torso is nude from the waist up except for jewels. The hands perform the *dharmacakramudrā*, which is supposed to represent the preaching of the First Sermon. The attendants, both female, are Tārābharikutī and Tārākurukulā.

Judging from the style we believe this bronze must have been made in Peninsular Thailand. It was discovered in Northeastern Thailand, but it is small enough to be carried from one place to another easily. Some scholars have suggested it was made in India in the Pāla period (eighth–twelfth century).

See Coedès, "Note sur une statuette bouddhique de style indojavanais provenant du Siam oriental," *Feestbundel uitgegevan door het Koninklijk Bataviaasch Genootschap van Kunsten en Wetenschappen . . .* , vol. 1 (Weltevreden, 1929), pp. 53–56.

22   Elephant

Dvāravatī style, 8th–11th century (?)
Terra cotta; H. 6½ in. (16.5 cm.)
National Museum, Û Tòng

This elephant, discovered at the village of Û Tòng, may have been made as an offering to a spirit shrine, a practice which survives to the present day in Thailand. (Not illustrated.)

57

23   Viṣṇu

Śrī Deb style, 9th century (?)
Stone; H. *82 ⁹⁄₁₆ in. (209 cm.)*
National Museum, Bangkok

This statue was discovered at Śrī Deb in the province of Petchabûn (Bejrapūrṇa), a site where several other statues of Hindu gods have come to light. The headdress is approximately cylindrical, but flattened in front. The god originally had four arms. He stands in a rather stiff triple flexion (*tribhaṅga*), and wears a short waistcloth, the end of which is tucked up at the back. The legs display a degree of anatomical realism; the neck, of exaggerated thickness, appears to be unfinished.

Publ.: Coedès, "Note sur quelques sculptures provenant de Śrīdeb (Siam)," in *Études d'orientalisme à la mémoire de Raymonde Linossier,* 2 vols. (Paris, 1932), pp. 159–164; Louis Frédéric, *Sud-est asiatique . . .,* fig. 261.

24   The Bodhisattva Avalokiteśvara

Śrīvijaya style, 9th–10th century
Bronze; H. *24 in. (61 cm.)*
National Museum, Gampèng Pet

Pun Pin in Peninsular Thailand, where this bronze was discovered, was apparently the site of an important town in the Śrīvijaya period. Traces of brick monuments and many bronze images have been unearthed there. This figure of Avalokiteśvara, identifiable by the figurine of Amitābha in his headdress, presumably belongs to the middle period of Śrīvijayan art. The hair and ears are stylized, and the body, though retaining something of the Indian conception of beauty, is rather stiff.

25   Standing Buddha Flanked by a Pair of Divinities

Dvāravatī style, 9th–10th century
Stone; H. 17 5/16 *in.* (44 *cm.*)
National Museum, Bangkok

This small relief was discovered at the Pathamacetiya, Nagara Paṭhama (see No. 18). The Buddha stands with his right hand in the posture known to Indian iconography as *vitarkamudrā* (gesture of exposition), while the posture of his left hand is difficult to decipher. Behind his head is an aureole carved with the elliptical and rectangular motifs, often seen in Dvāravatī art, which derive from Indian patterns of the Gupta or Post-Gupta period. He wears the monastic robe in the covering mode with the usual inflections.

The divinities accompanying the Buddha wear tall pointed crowns, and each carries a lotus and a fly-whisk (*cāmara*). It is impossible to say who they are supposed to be. As their crowns, dress, and attributes are identical they cannot be Indra and Brahmā, the gods shown in some Dvāravatī reliefs of the same type; neither is there any reason to suppose that this scene represents the Descent from the Tāvatiṃsa Heaven.

The Buddha and the two divinities stand on the head of a mythical beast which some Thai scholars call Vanaspati, the "Lord of the Forest." It has a bull's horns, the remains of a garuḍa's beak, and the wings of a haṃsa, the animals commonly ridden by Śiva, Viṣṇu, and Brahmā respectively. It has been suggested that this type of iconography, which has not been reported in India, was an invention of Dvāravatī art intended to show the superiority of Buddhism to Hinduism. This ingenious theory remains to be proved.

Near the middle of this relief, as in others, a hole has been bored, and there is a tenon at the back, intended to affix the piece within an architectural composition.

See Dhanit Yupho, *Brahmā with Four Faces* (Bangkok, 1967), fig. 6.

26   Female Musicians

Dvāravatī style, 9th–10th century
Stucco; H. 26 9/16 *in.* (67.5 *cm.*)
National Museum, Bangkok

This relief was discovered in the ruins of a monument outside the town of Kû Bua near Râtburî (Rājapurī). The musicians have facial features resembling those of the Dvāravatī native type, and wear earrings of Dvāravatī style (real earrings of this sort, made of metal, have been recovered from Dvāravatī sites). The first musician was probably holding a musical instrument, now lost. The second appears to be a singer. The third holds a vīṇā or "Indian lute" and the fourth a pair of percussion instruments, perhaps cymbals. The fifth is thought to be holding a stringed instrument, of a sort still used in Northeastern Thailand, with a sound-box made of a gourd, now lost; or else it might be a flute.

27   Jātaka Scene

Dvāravatī style, 9th–11th century
Stucco; H. 21¼ in. (54 cm.)
National Museum, Bangkok

These figures, from the base of a stupa at Kók Mai Dén in Nagara Svarga province, were part of a relief whose background has disappeared. The composition is thought to represent the Chaddanta-jātaka, a story of one of the Buddha's past lives when he was born as an elephant. A hunter is facing him.

Publ.: Dhanit Yupho, *Porāṇavatthusthāna samaya Dvāravatī hèn hmäi* [Some recently discovered sites of the Dvāravatī period], trans. A. B. Griswold (Bangkok, 1965), illustrated.

28   Head

Late Dvāravatī style, 9th–11th century (?)
Stucco; H. 17½ *in.* (44.5 *cm.*)
National Museum, Û Tòng

The identity of the personage to whom this head belonged is uncertain. The most conspicuous feature is the wide-open eyes, which are thought to indicate "rapt attention." Certain terra cotta figures of Buddhist disciples of the school of Haripuñjaya (Lampûn in Northern Thailand) have this feature, presumably because the disciples are listening with rapt attention to the Buddha's words. Some Dvāravatī demoniac gate-guardians (*dvārapālas*) wear similar expressions, denoting alertness in the performance of their duties, but they have other demon-like characteristics as well—such as a fierce aspect and protruding fangs—which are lacking in this head. The diadem suggests that the head belonged to some royal personage, human or divine, in process of being converted to the Doctrine and listening to the Buddha's exposition with eager delight.

The eyebrows are typical of the middle and late Dvāravatī styles. As the site of Û Tòng, where the head was discovered, was abandoned in the eleventh century, it seems impossible to give the head a later date.

29   Buddha Sheltered by the Nāga's Hood

Lopburî style, 11th century (?)
Stone; H. 46 ¹⁄₁₆ in. (117 cm.)
National Museum, Bangkok

Discovered in Burîram (Purīramya) Province, the statue is more or less typical of the Khmer style of the Baphuon.

Six of the Nāga's heads look up toward the main head, which as usual is at the top of the hood. The Buddha has a smooth, round ushnisha without a finial. The eyebrows, eyes, moustache, and beard were inlaid with some other material, which has now disappeared. The robe, which is in the open mode, is almost imperceptible except for the reserve of cloth between the left arm and the body, and the hem over the left wrist. (For the iconography of the subject, see p. 25.)

30 The Buddha of Grahi

Late Śrīvijaya style, A.D. 1183
Bronze; H. 64¹⁵/₁₆ *in. (165 cm.)*
National Museum, Bangkok

The "Buddha of Grahi" was discovered at Wat Wieng at Chaiyâ in Peninsular Thailand. The casting is in three separate parts: the Nāga's hood, the Buddha, and the Nāga's coils together with a rectangular base underneath, which bears an inscription giving a date equivalent to 1183. The Buddha is seated in the posture of "subduing Māra" rather than in "meditation," which is the one usually associated with the sixth week after his Enlightenment, when he was sheltered by the Nāgarāja. Some scholars have suggested that the image of the Buddha might be of later date than the rest of the composition; but the three parts fit together so well that it is impossible to believe they were made at different times. Perhaps the statue is intended to be a conflation of the first and sixth weeks following the Enlightenment.

The Buddha sits with folded legs, as in Khmer art, rather than with crossed legs as is usual in Śrīvijayan. His ushnisha is smooth and approximately hemispherical, with a flame-fringed bodhi leaf and "jewel" in front. The squareness of the face may reflect a Khmer heritage, but the facial features are more Śrīvijayan. The left palm is marked with the Wheel of the Doctrine. The monastic robe is worn in the open mode, with a shoulder-flap whose pleats are shown in anamorphosis.

The snouts of the serpent heads recall those of the Khmer style of the Bayon (late twelfth–early thirteenth century). The largest head is, as usual, at the top of the hood, while the other six look up toward it. At each of the seven throats there is a necklace, and on each breast a "jewel-in-lotus" pattern. Both the front and rear of the hood are covered with scales, and the rear has a group of concentric circles in the middle. From here a line in relief, representing the serpent's spine, runs down to the coiled body underneath.

Intervening between the Buddha's legs and the topmost coil of the Nāga's body is a cushion (?) with three narrow bands (one plain and two marked with lotus stamens), punctuated at the middle and at either side by a large, fully-opened lotus inlaid with colored glass, and below these bands a sloping area marked with concentric rows of small leaves (?). The three coils, with the spine outward, are covered with scales. Between the first and second coils, and again between the second and third, is another large fully-opened lotus. Between the bottom coil and the inscribed base is a single lotus petal, which looks as if it were part of still another fully-opened lotus most of which is hidden behind the base. All these lotus flowers and stamens help to emphasize the aquatic nature of the Nāgarāja, who lived in a pool bearing the same name as himself, Mucalinda. At the rear his tail may be seen writhing upward. (For the iconography, see p. 25.)

Publ.: Coedès, "À propos de la chute du royaume de Çrīvijaya," *Bijdragen tot de Taal-, Land-, en Volkenkunde van Nederlandsch-Indië* 83 (1927): 459–472; Dupont, "Le Buddha de Grahi et l'école de C'aiyâ," *Bulletin de l'École Française d'Extrême-Orient* 42 (1942): 105–113; *The Arts of Thailand* (Bloomington, 1960), p. 71, pl. 38; Coedès, *Recueil des inscriptions du Siam*, vol. 2, 2nd ed. (Bangkok, 1961), pp. 29–31 French section, pp. 32, 33 Siamese section; J. G. de Casparis, "The Date of the Grahi Buddha," *Journal of the Siam Society* 55 (1967): 31–40.

31   Torso of a Goddess

Style of Angkor Wat, first half of the 12th century
Stone; H. 38 9/16 in. (98 cm.)
Râm Kamhèng National Museum, Sukhodaya

This torso is one of a group of five statues of Hindu divinities discovered in the ruins of the Sāla Devarakṣa at Sukhodaya. According to Professor Boisselier, this shrine was built in the reign of Sūryavarman II of Cambodia (first half of the twelfth century) and the statues are contemporary with it. They are important because relatively few examples of sculpture in the round are known from this particular period. They allow us to see, at the backs of the figures, details of costume and jewelry which are visible only from the front in the bas-reliefs of goddesses in the temple of Angkor Wat.

Publ.: Boisselier, *Le Cambodge*, Manuel d'archéologie d'Extrême-Orient, pt. 1: Asie du Sud-Est, vol. 1 (Paris, 1966), p. 256 n. 1.

32   Divinity of Terrifying Aspect

Khmer or Khmerizing style, 12th century
Bronze; H. 6 ⁹⁄₁₆ in. (16 cm.)
National Museum, Bangkok

This figurine was discovered in the precinct of the Khmer Buddhist temple of Pimâi (Bimāya),
near Kórât, which was associated with Tāntric Mahāyāna Buddhism. The frowning eyebrows, protruding eyes, and two long fangs are marks of the divinity's "terrifying" aspect, often seen in
Tāntric iconography. His hair is dressed with a chignon on top. He wears earrings not unlike those
of Dvāravatī style, as well as a necklace, decorated belt, armlets, and bracelets of matching design.
His *sampot* or waist-cloth has a butterfly motif in the rear, which suggests some connection with
the Khmer style of the Baphuon (eleventh century). The right foot is a replacement. The original
pedestal, now missing, probably bore the figure of a corpse on which the divinity was dancing.

Divinities of this sort, dancing on corpses, are well known in Tāntric sculpture (cf. No. 35);
indeed one of them is represented on the lintel over the east door of the central tower of the Pimâi
temple, so the identification seems fairly certain. Some scholars call this bronze a dancing Māra;
but as no other images of such a subject are known, the theory seems fanciful.

33   Seated Crowned Buddha

Lopburî style, 12th–13th century
Bronze; H. 8¹⁵⁄₁₆ in. (22.7 cm.)
National Museum, Bangkok

The Buddha wears the monastic robe in the open mode, but the cloth between the left arm and the body has been eliminated. He also wears a diadem, crown (*mukuṭa*), earrings, necklace, armlets, bracelets, and anklets, all typical of the Khmer style of Angkor Wat (twelfth century). He sits in meditation, holding a round object which is thought to be the symbol of Bhaiṣajyaguru, the Healing Buddha.

34   Plaque with Buddhist Scenes

Lopburî style, 13th–14th century
Bronze; H. 6½ in. (16.5 cm.)
National Museum, Bangkok

The plaque is held by a deity dressed in royal attire typical of the Khmer style of the Bayon (late twelfth–early thirteenth century). Each side of the plaque has a border of flames (or perhaps leaves). The principal figure on each side is the Buddha, wearing a monastic robe in the open mode, pointing to the Earth with his right hand in the posture associated with his victory over Māra, and holding a fan-shaped eye-screen in his left hand. This is believed to be the earliest representation of such an eye-screen in art. The Buddha on the obverse sits in a sanctuary tower of Khmer type, with the Bodhi tree behind it; below him are two registers containing six persons each. The scene on the other side (illustrated) is much the same, but the tower is replaced by a niche surmounted by Bodhi leaves, and the two registers below the Buddha contain four and six persons respectively.

It is doubtful whether these two scenes actually represent the Buddha's victory over Māra; at least the persons in the registers do not look like *dramatis personae* connected with that event but seem to be simply worshipers. Perhaps they are doing homage to the great statue called the "Lion of the Śākyas." This statue, which commemorated the victory over Māra, was placed in the Mahābodhi Temple at Bodhgayā, beside the Bodhi tree where the victory occurred.

Publ.: Boisselier, *Le Cambodge*, p. 336 n. 4; Coedès, *Les collections archéologiques...*, *Ars Asiatica* 12, pl. 27.

35   Hevajra

Khmer or Lopburî style, 12th–13th century
Bronze; H. 6½ in. (16.5 cm.)
National Museum, Bangkok

Hevajra, a divinity worshipped in the Tāntric development of the Mahāyāna, is here seen with eight heads and sixteen arms. He is dancing, and wears the royal attire. His sixteen hands seem to be performing the *vitarkamudrā* (gesture of exposition). His dancing posture is similar to that of Caṇḍālī (No. 38), and it must also celebrate a victory, since Hevajra is the Destroyer of the Four Māras.

See D[avid] L. Snellgrove, *The Hevajra-Tāntra: A Critical Study*, 2 parts, London Oriental Series, vol. 6 (London, 1959).

36 a,b,c Battle Standards

> *Khmer style, 10th century (a and b) and ca. 14th century (c)*
> *Bronze;* H. a. 10 ¹⁄₁₆ *in.* (25.5 *cm.*), b. 7 ¹⁄₁₆ *in.* (18 *cm.*), c. 9 ⁷⁄₁₆ *in.* (24 *cm.*)
> *James H. W. Thompson Collection, Bangkok*

These bronze figurines were originally used as battle standards; note the sockets by which they were fitted to the ends of staffs. Professor Boisselier has attributed the first two (a and b) to the third quarter of the tenth century, and the third (c) to an uncertain date, probably later than the thirteenth century. They are said to have been discovered in the province of Surin.

Publ.: Boisselier, *Le Cambodge*, p. 342; idem, "Note sur quelques bronzes khmers d'aspect insolite," in *Essays Offered to G. H. Luce . . .* , vol. 2 (Ascona, 1966) ed. Ba Shin, Jean Boisselier and A. B. Griswold, pp. 30–36; Warren, *House on the Klong*, p. 84, pl. 19.

37 a,b,c Dancing Figures

> *Khmer or Khmerizing style, date uncertain*
> *Bronze;* H. a,b. 4 ⁷⁄₁₆ *in.* (11 *cm.*); c. 2¾ *in.* (7 *cm.*)
> *National Museum, Bangkok*

Three fragments of a pedestal (?) discovered at Kālasindhu in Northeastern Thailand. The costumes are reminiscent of the Khmer Baphuon style of the eleventh century, but the postures are more like those of the style of Angkor Wat or the Bayon (twelfth and early thirteenth), though they might possibly be dated between the fourteenth and sixteenth centuries, in the Ayudhyā period.

No exact parallel with the poses of the traditional theatrical dance has been traced.

Cf. Dhanit Yupho, *The Preliminary Course of Training in Thai Theatrical Art*, 2nd ed. rev., Thailand Culture Series, no. 15 (Bangkok, 1954).

38   Caṇḍālī

Lopburî style, 13th–14th century
Bronze; H. 7½ in. (19 cm.)
James H. W. Thompson Collection, Bangkok

Caṇḍālī, a Tāntric Mahāyāna divinity, is one of eight goddesses known as Yoginīs and associated with Hevajra. Described as "dark like a cloud," and possessed of a third eye, she holds a discus in her right hand, and a plowshare across her breast. Like her sisters she is a Destroyer of Ignorance; hence her posture is that of a dance of victory. The image was found in Kórât province.

Boeles says that the plow she holds in her left hand is of a shape still in use today to prepare flooded fields for the planting of rice.

Publ.: J. J. Boeles, "Two Yoginīs of Hevajra from Thailand," in *Essays Offered to G. H. Luce*, vol. 2, pp. 14–29; Warren, *House on the Klong*, p. 84, pl. 25.

39   Viṣṇu

Khmer or Khmerizing style, 13th–14th century
Bronze; H. 3½ in. (8.8 cm.)
National Museum, Bangkok

Evidently the god originally rode on the Garuḍa or sun-bird, which is now missing. As in the style of Angkor Wat (first half of the twelfth century) he stood on the bird's shoulders, with his legs slightly bent in the attitude of combat. See Boisselier, "Garuḍa dans l'art khmèr," *Bulletin de l'École Française d'Extrême-Orient* 44 (1947–1950): 67. His dress is typical of the Bayon and post-Bayon styles. He holds the discus in his upper right hand, the lotus in his lower right; the conch was doubtless in the lost upper left hand, and the club was in the lower left.

40   Standing Buddha

Lopburî style, 13th–14th century
Bronze; H. 7⅞ *in. (20 cm.)*
National Museum, Bangkok

At times during the period from the early eleventh to the late thirteenth century Lopburî was a stronghold of Khmer power in Thailand; its art was in large part a reflection of that of Cambodia and even after the withdrawal of the Khmer rulers the tradition persisted.

Here the two-tiered ushnisha and its finial form a low cone. The hair is arranged in vertical tresses, separated from the forehead by two narrow bands and from the nape of the neck by one. The face, square and austere, is reminiscent of the Khmer style of Angkor Wat (first half of the twelfth century). The posture represents a survival of the Dvāravatī type, with the hands held in a position similar to No. 5. The palms are marked with the Wheel of the Doctrine.

The Buddha wears the robe in the covering mode with the U-inflection, rendered in partial anamorphosis. Some elements of the royal attire are added: the necklace is hung on top of the robe, while the belt, decorated with pendants typical of the Khmer styles of Angkor Wat and the Bayon, belongs to the undercloth but is seen through the conventional "transparency" of the robe. Shown in the same manner is the frontal panel that runs down the center of the undercloth.

There is something odd about the part of the undercloth seen hanging below the bottom of the robe. While the central portion of it is correctly shown, hanging down between the front and rear portions of the robe, the corners at left and right appear to be stuck on behind the rear hem, which is a manifest impossibility. If this is not due to repairs, it is one of the rather rare instances in which an image-maker was guilty of a flagrant mistake. The ivory pedestal is modern.

On the Buddha's back is a perforated tenon, to which an aureole, now lost, was probably attached.

79

41   Crowned Buddha

Lopburî style, 13th–14th century
Bronze; H. 8⅜ in. (21.2 cm.)
James H. W. Thompson Collection, Bangkok

This figure represents the Buddha in the posture of subduing Māra. In addition to the monastic dress he wears several of the ornaments of royalty—a diadem with a succession of tall peaks, long earrings that fall to the shoulders, a necklace, and armlets. The design of the diadem, and some of the other ornaments, recall the art of the latter part of the Indian Pāla style (tenth–twelfth century), as may the triangular *ūrṇā* in the forehead. Other characteristics, such as the pointed ushnisha-cover, the facial features, the necklace, the type of monastic robe, and the posture, with legs folded, are more in the Khmer style. The top and sides of the base are decorated with intricate patterns of lotus petals and stamens. The tenons under the base show that it originally stood on top of another pedestal. At the Buddha's back is a perforated tenon, the purpose of which was doubtless to attach an aureole that is now lost.

   This image is said to have been discovered in Lopburî province. An approximate date may be provided by a very similar image discovered in the crypt of Wat Râtbûrana (Rājapūraṇaḥ) at Ayudhyā, built in 1424.

Publ.: Warren, *House on the Klong,* p. 86, pl. 68.

42   Buddha Sheltered by the Nāga's Hood

Lopburî style, 13th–14th century
Bronze; H. *20½ in. (52 cm.)*
Collection of Prince Piyarangsit, Bangkok

This Buddha image is of a type which derives from those produced, in considerable numbers, in the Khmer style of the Bayon (late twelfth–early thirteenth century). It is cast in three separate pieces: the Buddha, the coiled body of the Nāga, and the Nāga's hood. The casting is a superb piece of work. (For the iconography, see p. 25.)

Publ.: Diskul, *Masterpieces from Private Collections,* pp. 12, 13, pl. 20.

43   Head from a Buddha Image

"Û Tòng B" style, 13th–14th century
Bronze; H. 24 7/16 in. (62 cm.)
National Museum, Ayudhyā

44   Head from a Buddha Image

"Û Tòng B" style, 13th–14th century
Bronze; H. 11 13/16 in. (30 cm.)
National Museum, Bangkok

These heads must be approximately contemporary. One has lost its ushnisha, and both have lost the finials, which were undoubtedly in the form of a flame. Apart from the size of the curls the differences between them are not very conspicuous. Both have square faces and austere expressions typical of the "Û Tòng B" style with its numerous heritages from the Khmerizing art of Lopburî.

The "Û Tòng" style (which has nothing to do with the place now named Û Tòng; see Appendix B, p. 134) is typical of the sculpture of the Ayudhyā region from the thirteenth century or earlier to about the middle of the fifteenth. It is usually subdivided into three groups, A, B, and C, which probably succeeded one another in that order, but of course with some overlapping. Griswold, who first proposed this classification, placed the so-called Û Tòng images that most resemble those of the Dvāravatī style in group A, those with Khmer-style faces in group B, and those with oval faces in group C.

See *The Arts of Thailand*, p. 141.

45   Buddha in Meditation

Lopburî style, 13th–14th century
Stone; H. 39⅜ in. (100 cm.)
National Museum, Bangkok

The Buddha sits in meditation on a lotus throne. The ushnisha-cover is ornamented with lotus petals and surmounted by a finial in the form of a "jewel." The large curls are separated from the forehead by a brow-band and on the forehead is a very small circular *ūrṇā*. The square face has a smiling expression typical of the Khmer style of the Bayon (late twelfth–early thirteenth century). The robe is worn in the open mode with the reversing inflection and the shoulder-flap of the robe seems to be hidden by a folded shawl (*saṅghāṭi*) laid on top of it. Like the majority of images of the Buddha in Thailand, this statue, found at Lopburî, was originally lacquered and gilded. Traces of lacquer still adhere to it.

     Publ.: Coedès, *Les collections archéologiques . . . , Ars Asiatica* 12, pl. 21.

46   Head from a Buddhist Statue

Lopburî style, 13th–14th century
Stone; H. 20 1/16 in. (51 cm.)
National Museum, Bangkok

The back of the head, which was discovered in the precinct of the temple of the Great Relic (Mahādhātu) at Lopburî, has a fracture which suggests that it belonged to a statue of the Buddha sheltered by the Nāgarāja's hood (cf. No. 30). The features, however, recall those of Khmer statues of Prajñāparamitā, a female Bodhisattva of the Khmer pantheon, carved in the style of the Bayon.

Publ.: Coedès, *Les collections archéologiques . . . , Ars Asiatica* 12, pl. 30.

47   Buddha Subduing Māra

"Û Tòng A" or "B" style, 13th–14th century
Bronze; H. 9 1/16 in. (23 cm.)
National Museum, Ayudhyā

This Buddha was discovered in the crypt of the main *prāṅg* of Wat Râtbûrana (Rājapūraṇaḥ) at Ayudhyā, which was built in 1424. This date is therefore the *terminus ante quem* for the image; but how old it was when it was placed in the crypt is uncertain. Depending on how the subdivisions are defined, this image may be placed in either the "Û Tòng A" or "B" group. According to Griswold's system of classification however, it would be assigned to Group B.

The conical ushnisha-cover is studded with small lotus petals, set with slightly larger floral motifs, and surmounted by a finial in the form of a jewel. The floral motifs, the band separating the hair from the forehead, and the shape and expression of the face, all recall the Khmerizing art of Lopburî. The form of the pedestal suggests an early stage in the development of the typical "Û Tòng" pedestal as seen in No. 49.

48   Reclining Buddha   *(illustrated p. 21)*

"Û Tòng A" or "B" style, 13th–14th century
Bronze; L. 15⅜ in. (39 cm.)
National Museum, Bangkok

The Buddha reclines on his right side, with his head resting on his right hand, which in turn rests on a pillow. The four-legged couch he lies on is his deathbed, for he is entering *parinibbāna*. An adoring disciple kneels at his feet. The difference in size between the two figures expresses the difference in their importance. On the front of the couch is an inscription which has not yet been deciphered.

This image was excavated recently by the Department of Fine Arts at the temple of the Great Relic (Mahādhātu) at Ayudhyā.

90

49   Buddha Subduing Māra

"Û Tòng B" style, c. 14th century
Bronze; H. 12 ⁹⁄₁₆ *in.* (31 *cm.*)
National Museum, Bangkok

This image was found at Gampèng Pet (Kāṃbèṅ Bejra) southwest of Sukhodaya. A very similar
image from the same place has been attributed by Griswold to the reign of Mahādharmarājā III of
Sukhodaya (c. 1398–1419), who was reduced to vassalage by Ayudhyā. According to Griswold's
surmise, the conquerors commissioned numerous sculptors in the Sukhodaya region to cast images
in the style which then prevailed at Ayudhyā. (See A. B. Griswold, *Towards a History of Sukhodaya
Art* [Bangkok, 1967], p. 52.)

The finial on the ushnisha has the form of a flame composed of five jets joined together. The
hair, consisting of small curls, is separated from the forehead by a band. The square, austere face
recalls the Khmerizing art of Lopburî. As is frequently the case in the "Û Tòng" styles, the upper
edge of the undercloth, seen through the transparency of the robe, is shown in conspicuous relief.
The form of the pedestal is typical of the developed "Û Tòng" style.

50   Guardian Figure

Sukhodaya style, c. 14th century
Glazed ceramic; H. 41³⁄₈ *in.* (105 *cm.*)
National Museum, Bangkok

This figure, discovered in the ruins of Sukhodaya, was probably made at the kilns just north of the
town. The demoniac features, as well as the position of the hands which probably held a club,
indicate that this was a door-guardian (*dvārapāla*). The costume is typical of the Sukhodaya period,
showing lingering influences from the art of Cambodia or Lopburî.

51   Divinities in Adoration

Sukhodaya style, 14th century
Stucco on a brick armature; H. 22 ⁷⁄₁₆ *in. (57 cm.)*
National Museum, Bangkok

This fragment of a relief comes from the ruins of a stupa or vihāra at Wat Pra Pâi Luang, Sukhodaya. The divinities may be spectators remaining in the Tāvatiṃsa Heaven while the Buddha descends to earth, or else doing homage to him in some other scene from his life. Those in the upper register wear tall Thai crowns and a profusion of jewelry, but sit in a posture that reminds us of Khmer art. Those in the lower register wear diadems.

52   Harihara

Sukhodaya style, 14th century
Bronze; H. 48 *in. (122 cm.)*
National Museum, Bangkok

The Hindu god Harihara combines Viṣṇu and Śiva in a single body. Here the disk and conch, attributes of Viṣṇu, are held in the upper right and left hands, while the vertical third eye on the forehead and the serpent on the Brahmanical cord over the shoulder are typical of Śiva.

It is not surprising that Hindu images were cast at Sukhodaya, although the king and the people were fervent Buddhists. Numerous state ceremonies had to be performed by Hindu priests, and every court in Southeast Asia had Brahmin advisors. Even now some ceremonies at the court of Thailand are performed by Brahmins.

Publ.: Diskul, *Devarūpa samṛddhi samaya Sukhodaya* (Bangkok, 1966), *passim.*

93

53   Footprint of the Buddha   *(illustrated p. 14)*

Sukhodaya style, 14th century
Bronze; L. 61 ⁷⁄₁₆ in. (156 cm.)
National Museum, Bangkok

A frieze of "walking" Buddhas of the Past is engraved on the top register of this bronze, discovered at Wat Sadet (Stec) in the town of Gampèng Pet (Kāṃbèṅ Bejra) and supposed to be a replica of the footprint left by the Buddha himself on Adam's Peak in Ceylon. At the side are world-guardians, dressed in Sukhodayan costumes and carrying swords; at the bottom are Buddhist disciples carrying lotuses. An inscription in Siamese, written in Khmer letters, supports these identifications. The Wheel of the Doctrine, surrounded by 108 auspicious symbols, is seen at the left. (For the legend of the Buddha's Footprint see Appendix C, p. 135; for Gampèng Pet see No. 62.)

54   Standing Buddha   *(illustrated p. 24)*

"Û Tòng B" style, 14th or early 15th century
Gold repoussé; H. 7½ in. (19 cm.)
National Museum, Ayudhyā

This image was discovered in the crypt of Wat Rātbûrana (Rājapūraṇaḥ), Ayudhyā. The Buddha wears the monastic robe in the covering mode. Seen through its transparency are the richly ornamented belt and frontal panel of the undercloth, which are part of royal attire rather than of monastic dress. The right hand is raised in the posture known to Indian iconography as "dispelling fear"; what its significance was in medieval Thailand is not known. The palm of the hand is marked with the Wheel of the Doctrine.

55   Fragment of a Head from a Statue of the Buddha

Northern Thailand style, 14th–15th century
Bronze; H. 24 in. (61 cm.)
National Museum, Lampûn

This fragment was discovered in a ruin at Lampûn. The large curls, self-satisfied expression, and replete forms of the face recall those of numerous "Lion type" images from Northern Thailand (see No. 64). The chin and the ear-tops are like those frequently seen in the art of Sukhodaya from the fourteenth century and later. The oval line marking the chin, so often found in the classic and post-classic art of Sukhodaya, is an interpretation of the simile in classical Indian poetry which describes a hero's chin as "like a mango stone."

96

56   Votive Tablet

Sukhodaya style, late 14th or early 15th century
Lead; H. 12⅜ *in.* (31.5 cm.)
National Museum, Bangkok

This plaque was discovered in the crypt of Wat Râtbûrana. At the top is a two-tiered honorific parasol, above an arched doorway supported by a pair of columns with vases of flowers placed in front of them. (See p. 23.)

The figure represents the "walking" Buddha or, to be more precise, the Buddha who has just paused in the act of walking. His left foot is planted firmly on the ground, while his right heel is raised. His left hand is held upward, his right hangs at his side. In some Sukhodaya stucco reliefs this is the posture of the Buddha in the Descent from the Tāvatiṃsa Heaven (see Griswold, *Towards a History of Sukhodaya Art*, pls. 42a, 43), but in another he is shown in the same posture in a different episode (ibid., pl. 42b).

The robe is worn in the open mode. Note the long arms, flat footsoles, and projecting heels of the "supernatural anatomy."

57   "Walking" Buddha

Sukhodaya style, 14th–15th century
Bronze; H. 3¹⁵⁄₁₆ *in.* (10 cm.)
National Museum, Bangkok

Though the "walking" Buddha is represented in bas-reliefs in India and at Pagán in Burma, as well as in paintings in Ceylon, the school of Sukhodaya was apparently the first to produce images in the round of the Buddha in this posture. The subject involves difficult sculptural problems which the author of this image has not solved very successfully.

The iconography of the figure is much the same as in No. 56. Through the conventional "transparency" of the robe, the top of the undercloth can be seen at the waist.

Cf. *The Arts of Thailand* pls. 72, 81, 86 for examples of successful treatment of the subject.

58 a,b　　Hands from Images of the Buddha

Sukhodaya style, 14th or 15th century
Bronze; Right hand, H. *5⅞ in. (15 cm.)*
Left hand, H. *7⅞ in. (20 cm.)*
National Museum, Gampèng Pet

These graceful hands, discovered in the ruins of Sukhodaya, are in the posture known to Indian iconography as *abhayamudrā*, the gesture of dispelling fear. In the art of Sukhodaya, in which the significance of the gesture is not necessarily the same, the "walking" Buddha usually raises his left hand in this posture (particularly when he is shown descending from the Tāvatiṃsa Heaven), while the other hand hangs alongside the leg. But examples of the converse are not infrequent (cf. Griswold, *Towards a History of Sukhodaya Art*, pls. 42a–45, with the left hand raised; ibid. pl. 55b, with the right hand raised).

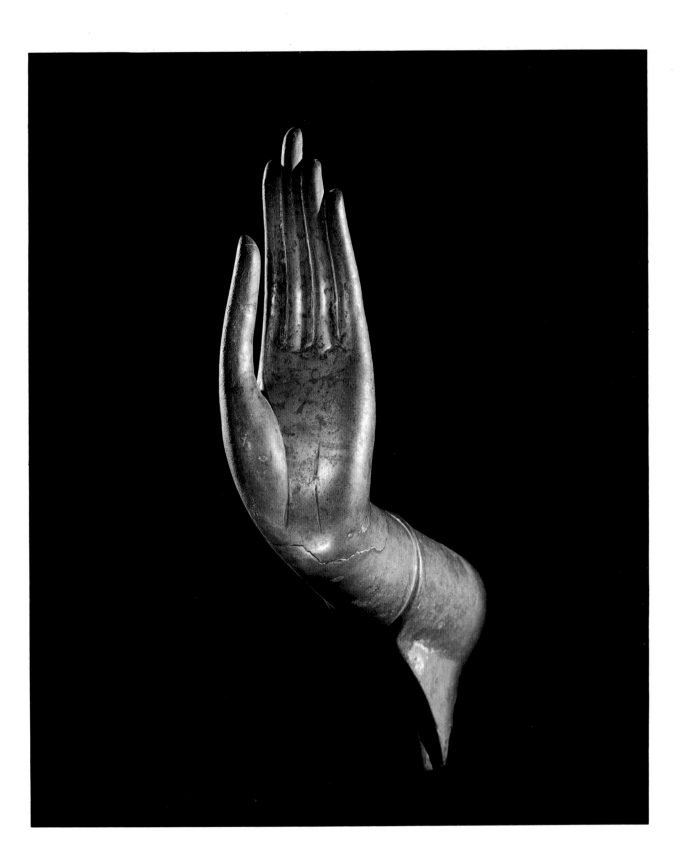

59   Buddha Subduing Māra

Sukhodaya style, 14th or 15th century
Bronze; H. 47⅝ in. (121 cm.)
National Museum, Ayudhyā

60   Buddha Subduing Māra

Sukhodaya style, 14th or 15th century
Bronze; H. 48 1⁄16 in. (122 cm.)
National Museum, Sukhodaya

As these two statues are both good examples of the Sukhodayan post-classic style, they may be considered together. The iconographic differences between them are minute. Both are rendered in highly stylized modeling which gives plastic interpretation to the similes used in classical Indian poetic descriptions of heroes: the nose like a parrot's beak, the chin like a mango stone, arms firm and rounded like the trunk of an elephant, fingers like the petals of a lotus that is just beginning to open, and so on. No illusion of reality is intended.

See *The Arts of Thailand*, pp. 90–99.

60. Buddha Subduing Māra;
head (opposite) and other details.

103

61   Head from a Buddha Image

Sukhodaya style, late 14th or 15th century
Bronze; H. 24⅝ in. (62.5 cm.)
National Museum, Bangkok

This bronze was discovered at Wat Araññika (the name denotes an establishment of "forest-dwelling" monks) near Biṣṇuloka. The ushnisha has lost its finial, which doubtless had the form of a flame, and the ear lobes have been broken off. This head and No. 62 are splendidly representative of a conventional style which seeks to translate into plastic terms the commonplace metaphors of Sanskrit poetry. (See entry No. 55.)

62   Head from a Buddha Image

Post-classic school of Sukhodaya, 14th–15th century
Bronze; H. 30 ⁵⁄₁₆ *in. (77 cm.)*
National Museum, Bangkok

The town of Gampèng Pet, on the Ping river southwest of Sukhodaya, enjoyed its greatest prosperity from the fifteenth to the seventeenth century. Though it was by this time part of the kingdom of Ayudhyā, many of its artists carried on the traditions of Sukhodaya which had been handed down to them by their teachers. In most respects this head would be difficult to distinguish from the contemporaneous work of Sukhodaya itself, though the shape of the face, narrowing downward markedly from the broad forehead, is said to be typical of the Gampèng Pet (Kāmbèṅ Bejra) sub-school.

63   Buddha Subduing Māra

"Û Tòng C" style, late 14th or 15th century
Bronze; H. *33 ¹⁄₁₀ in. (84 cm.)*
National Museum, Chainât (Jayanāda)

This image from Chainât (Jayanāda) in central Thailand is similar to an image of "Û Tòng C" style found in the ruins of Sukhodaya, which Griswold attributes to the reign of Mahādharmarājā IV (1419–38) who ruled over Sukhodaya as a vassal of Ayudhyā (see Griswold, *Towards a History of Sukhodaya Art,* p. 55, pl. 57b).

The finial on the ushnisha is lost, but it must have been similar to that of the image from Sukhodaya, in the form of a flame with several jets undulating upward (No. 60). Typical of the "Û Tòng C" style are the small curls, the narrow band separating the hair from the forehead, the oval face, the arrangement of the monastic robe, and, doubtless, the pedestal (of which only the upper half survives).

The "Û Tòng C" style was probably at its height in the 1420's. The greatest number of images found in the crypt of Wat Râtbûrana, built in 1424, are of this style. About 300 of them were found in this crypt, and it may be assumed that they were cast expressly to be placed there as an act of merit.

64   Buddha Subduing Māra

Sukhodaya style or Northern Thailand style, c. 15th century (?)
Bronze; H. 36¼ *in. (92 cm.)*
National Museum, Chainât (Jayanāda)

This image, which was discovered at Chainât, is of the "Lion" type. The iconography, which stems ultimately from some Indian prototype of the Pāla period (eighth–twelfth century), doubtless the famous statue at Bodhgayā called Śākyasiṅha, "the Lion of the Śākyas," is clearly established; the finial on the ushnisha represents a jewel shaped like a lotus bud; the monastic robe is worn in the open mode, with a shoulder-flap that ends in a notched motif above the nipple; the legs are crossed in the posture known as *vajrāsana* (the "adamantine pose"); the right hand is in the attitude of "calling the Earth to witness" or "subduing Māra."

Many images of this type were cast in Northern Thailand and several bear inscriptions with dates between 1470 and 1555, but Professor Boisselier believes a few undated sculptures are from the early fourteenth century. Several were also produced by the School of Sukhodaya, at dates which remain to be determined. Sometimes, as here, it is difficult to decide which of the two schools may have created an image of the "Lion" type.

65   Buddha Subduing Māra

"Û Tòng C" style (?), early 15th century
Crystal; H. 2 9/16 *in. (6.5 cm.)*
National Museum, Ayudhyā

This image comes from the crypt of Wat Râtbûrana, built in 1424 (see No. 63). Originally the figure may have had gold fittings, such as an ushnisha-cover, which would perhaps have made the style more apparent. If the image was made at Ayudhyā for enshrinement in the crypt, we should expect the style to be "Û Tòng C." On the other hand it may have come from Northern Thailand. (Not illustrated.)

66 a,b,c Three Votive Plaques   *(illustrated p. 28)*

> a, b. *"Û Tòng C" style, early 15th century*
> *Gold repoussé; a. H. 2⅜ in. (6 cm.); b. H. 2¾ in. (7 cm.)*
> *National Museum, Ayudhyā*

These plaques were discovered in the same crypt as No. 65. The subject is the Buddha seated under the Bodhi tree, subduing Māra. They were made by the repoussé method from a die. Some confusion has occurred between right and left—in both images the Buddha's monastic robe, worn in the open mode, covers his right shoulder instead of his left, which is quite unheard-of; the left leg is folded on top of the right one, which is unusual though not unknown. Yet the right hand rests on the knee in the orthodox manner.

> c. *Ayudhyā style, 15th–16th century*
> *Gold repoussé; H. 3 1/16 in. (7.7 cm.)*
> *James H. W. Thompson Collection, Bangkok*

This plaque, which also shows the Buddha subduing Māra, is free of the error found in Nos. 66a,b. The Buddha is flanked by two disciples who are kneeling in adoration and holding flowers in their hands.

Publ.: Warren, *House on the Klong*, p. 84, pl. 33.

67 a,b,c,d Four Votive Plaques   *(illustrated p. 29)*

> *Ayudhyā style, 15th–16th century*
> *Gold repoussé;*
> a. *Elephant with a feathered tail;* H. 2 9/16 in. (6.5 cm.)
> b. *Horse with a feathered tail;* H. 3⅜ in. (8.5 cm.)
> c. *Elephant;* H. 3 5/16 in. (8.4 cm.)
> d. *Dancing figure;* H. 4⅛ in. (10.5 cm.)
> *National Museum, Ayudhyā*

Such plaques were commonly buried with other precious objects under the base of a *vihāra* or *uposatha* hall in a monastery, as auspicious devices.

68   "Walking" Buddha

> *Chaiyâ style, 15th–16th century (?)*
> *Bronze; H. 8½ in. (21.5 cm.)*
> *National Museum, Bangkok*

This bronze, discovered at the temple of the Great Relic (Mahādhātu) at Chaiyâ, has usually been ascribed either to the late Dvāravatī style of the tenth or eleventh century or to the school of Śrīvijaya (eighth–thirteenth century). The "walking" posture, however, appears to derive from the art of Sukhodaya of the late thirteenth–fifteenth century, while the arrangement of the undercloth, with its overhang at the waist and its frontal panel—though seen in some Sukhodayan images of the standing Buddha of the fourteenth (?) century—seems more closely related to the Ayudhyā style of the fifteenth. Hence our proposed dating, though the head shows some reminiscences of the style of Śrīvijaya.

Publ.: Dupont, *L'archéologie mône . . .*, pp. 225, 226, fig. 467.

69 a,b,c Three Reliquary Caskets

a. Reliquary Casket in the Form of a Deer

Northern Thailand style, 15th–18th century
Soapstone and gold; H. 1¹³⁄₁₆ *in.* (4.6 cm.)
National Museum, Bangkok

Several years ago, when the Bhūmibol Dam in Northwestern Thailand was being built, the Department of Fine Arts excavated numerous old monuments in the area which was destined to be flooded. This reliquary casket was found in one of them. The head of the crouching deer, turned toward the left, has a golden mask. The legs are also covered with gold. The cavity on the animal's back, intended to enshrine relics of the Buddha, has an elaborately decorated gold lid. (Not illustrated.)

b. Reliquary Casket in the Form of an Elephant

Northern Thailand style, 15th–18th century
Yellow stone; H. 1¹⁄₁₆ *in.* (2.7 cm.)
National Museum, Bangkok

The elephant, from a stupa north of the Bhūmibol Dam, Northwestern Thailand, is prostrating himself on the ground and raising his trunk in an attitude of homage. On his back is a cavity for relics of the Buddha, protected by a lid. (Not illustrated.)

c. Reliquary Casket

Northern Thailand style, 16th–17th century
Crystal; H. 6¹¹⁄₁₆ *in.* (17 cm.)
National Museum, Bangkok

The base of this reliquary, from the same area as No. 69b, is composed of four figures of the Buddha seated in the posture of subduing Māra. A figure of the standing Buddha forms the lid. The five figures doubtless represent the five Buddhas of the present aeon, four of whom have already passed into *parinibbāna*, while the fifth, Āriya Metteya (Sanskrit: Maitreya), is still to come. (Not illustrated.)

70   Lion with Two Bodies

Northern Thailand style, 15th–18th century
Bronze; H. 10¹³⁄₁₆ *in.* (27.5 cm.)
National Museum, Bangkok

The configuration of this bronze from Chieng Râi recalls the story in the Ceylon Chronicles about the Asokan missionaries who, when they arrived at Suvaṇṇabhūmi (see No. 4a), found a she-demon leaping out of the water to devour the ruler's newborn son. She was guarded by an army of imps, each in the form of a lion with two bodies joined to a single head. The monks quickly put the demon to flight by creating twice as many imps of similar aspect. Then they pronounced one of the Buddha's Discourses. Much relieved at the happy outcome, the ruler was converted to the Doctrine. See Griswold, "Burma" in *Burma-Korea-Tibet*, Art of the World (London, 1964), p. 13. (Not illustrated.)

71   Standing Buddha

Northern Thailand style, 16th–18th century
Bronze; H. *19½ in. (49.5 cm.)*
National Museum, Bangkok

The art of Northern Thailand from the fourteenth century to the present, centering at Chieng Mai, is commonly called "later Chieng Sèn art." In much of it there are reminiscences of the art of Sukhodaya (thirteenth–fifteenth century) and here the Sukhodayan influence is visible in the tall finial in the form of a flame, the small curls of hair, the oval face, and the arched eyebrows. The Buddha, wearing the robe in the covering mode, carries an almsbowl in both hands. The robe is pushed up along both forearms, forming heavy folds. The pedestal, with its lotus petals and stamens, is typical of Northern Thailand. Photographed before the library of Wat Phra Singh, Chieng Ma.

115

72   Trimūrti in Salutation (?)

Northern Thailand style, 16th–18th century
Bronze; H. 8⅝ in. (21.9 cm.)
National Museum, Bangkok

The accepted but unproven interpretation of this figure is that it represents Trimūrti, a fusion of the three great Hindu gods, Brahmā, Siva and Viṣṇu. The divinity has three faces, each topped by a diadem; the single head has a pyramidal crown with a small triangular protuberance behind each diadem, in the late Ayudhyā style. The figure has four arms, broad shoulders, and a thin waist, and the ornaments—necklace, armlets, and bracelets—are typical of those found on Ayudhyā images. The right and left front hands are in an attitude of salutation; the upper right seems to hold a conch, and the left a lotus, both attributes of Visnu.

73   Hermit

Northern Thailand style. Cast in 1604
Bronze; H. 29⅛ *in.* (74 *cm.*)
National Museum, Bangkok

This figure of a hermit, discovered at Chieng Sèn in the extreme north of Thailand, is seen seated
in *yogāsana* (the posture of a yogi), with hands raised in salutation. Around him are the requisites
of a hermit—a small kettle, a bowl, and a basket. Shown in relief on the oval base are a wooden
rod with two vases, a fire poker (?), a walking stick (?), a fly-whisk, a covered bowl on a tripod for
heating food, a saluting divinity, and a deer with reverted head. The rest of the base is covered with
an inscription in Pali and Thai, written in the characters of Northern Thailand, which states that
the ruler of Chieng Sèn had this image cast at a date equivalent to 1604 A.D. A carrying lug on the
base suggests that the bronze was sometimes taken outdoors for ceremonies.

74   Buddha in Meditation Beneath the Bodhi Tree

Ayudhyā style, 16th–18th century
Bronze; H. 14 in. (35.5 cm.)
National Museum, Bangkok

This bronze represents the Buddha just before his Enlightenment. The Bodhi tree in the rear was cast separately, whereas the Buddha and the base with its teeming figures are cast in a single piece.

The Buddha is rather corpulent. The finial on his ushnisha represents a jewel in the form of a lotus-bud. He is seated in meditation on a lotus and is wearing a monastic robe in the open mode. The base is crowded with hostile spirits who wish to prevent him from attaining Enlightenment. Helping them are some serpents, an elephant with two riders, and two monsters with bulls' heads. An elephant at the Buddha's left, however, seems to have given up already, as he is holding a lotus in his trunk in an act of worship, while the mahout on his back is also in a posture of homage.

The smaller lotus pedestal in front of the Buddha doubtless supported a figurine of the Earth-Goddess who came to help him by flooding out the hostile spirits with the water of merit squeezed from her hair.

75   Head of a Buddhist Monk

Ayudhyā style, 17th century
Terra cotta; H. 9 ¹⁄₁₆ *in. (23 cm.)*
National Museum, Ayudhyā

This head was transferred to the Ayudhyā Museum from the little museum at Bâng Rachan in the province of Singburî (Siṅhapurī). As there is no ushnisha, it cannot have belonged to an image of the Buddha, and so may be presumed to have belonged to a monk. The arching eyebrows, at an exaggerated distance from the eyes, are typical of seventeenth century art. (Not illustrated.)

76   Standing Buddha

Chaiyâ (Jaiyā) style, Peninsular Siam, 17th–18th century
Bronze; H. 12⅝ *in. (32 cm.)*
National Museum, Bangkok

The art of Śrīvijaya (eighth–thirteenth century), which was largely devoted to Mahāyāna Buddhism, established a tradition whose traces survived in Peninsular Siam for centuries after the fall of the kingdom of Śrīvijaya and the conversion of the region to Theravāda Buddhism. This image is said to have been discovered at Chaiyâ, and may date from the late Ayudhyā period.

The curls of hair are quite small. The ushnisha and finial merge together in the shape of a low cone. The face is rather square, perhaps a reminiscence of a Khmer or Lopburî type. The right hand is raised with thumb and forefinger joined (the *vitarkamudrā* of Indian iconography), while the left hand is lowered with the palm forward (the *varadamudrā* or "gesture of bestowing favors" in Indian iconography). In the Mahāyāna, according to Miss Alice Getty, this combination signifies preaching to the inhabitants of heaven, earth, and hell. The monastic robe is worn in the open mode, covering the left shoulder but leaving the right shoulder bare; an unusual feature is that it is pushed up high at the left, leaving most of that arm bare too.

Publ.: Dupont, "Le Buddha de Grahi . . . ," *Bulletin de l'École Française d'Extrême-Orient* 42, pp. 110, 111.

77   Kneeling Divinity

Ayudhyā style, 17th–18th century
Wood; H. 40 ⁹⁄₁₆ *in.* (102 *cm.*)
National Museum, Ayudhyā

Around November, at the end of the month-long annual retreat which coincides with the last part of the rainy season, there is a ceremonial presentation of robes to all the monasteries, a joyful occasion when everyone earns much merit. This wooden statue of a kneeling divinity with out-stretched hands was probably used in such ceremonies, as a stand to hold the set of robes which was to be presented to the most respected monk present. The divinity wears the royal attire with a profusion of jewels.

Cf. Boisselier, *La statuaire khmère et son évolution* (Saigon, 1955), pl. 85, for a comparable figure in the National Museum in Phnom-Penh.

78   Buddha Seated on a Mythical Animal

Northern Thailand, 17th–18th century
Bronze; H. 15⅜ in. (39 cm.)
National Museum, Bangkok

The Buddha, wearing a monastic robe in the open mode, sits in meditation on a lotus cushion placed on top of a mythical bird with an elephant's trunk. Certain elements of the design appear to have been inspired by Chinese example.

Publ.: Lucien Fournereau, *Le Siam ancien*, vol. 1 (Paris, 1895), pl. 35.

79   Pair of Door Panels with Guardian Figures

Ayudhyā style, 17th–18th century
Wood; H. 77 ⁹⁄₁₆ in. (196 cm.)
National Museum, Ayudhyā

Discovered at the entrance to one of the three large stupas of the Chapel Royal at Ayudhyā, which were built in the late fifteenth century, these panels must have been a later addition. The guardian figures are divinities sheltered by parasols decorated with garlands. Their jewelry is of the late Ayudhyā style, with reminiscences of the style of Cambodia or Lopburî.

80   Buddha Subduing Māra

Bangkok style, late 18th or 19th century
Bronze; H. 11¼ in. (28.2 cm.)
Property of His Majesty King Bhūmibol Adulyadej of Thailand

This image is a copy of the Victory Buddha of King Rāma I (r. 1782–1809). The Buddha, wearing a monastic dress decorated in gold, sits under a seven-tiered parasol which is part of the regalia of a crown prince (the Buddha never became a king). The simulated rug hanging over the pedestal is ornamented with jewelry which shows the remarkable skill of the Bangkok goldsmiths. All of the Buddha images of this period had the same insipid facial expression, but the details of the decoration were superb. An eye-screen to aid in meditation and, according to popular belief, to ward off all misfortunes, is normally held in the left hand but is here shown lying in front of the pedestal.

Fig. 4. Central portion of wall painting, "Calling the Earth to Witness," in Wat Chöng Tâ, Ayudhyā. Reproduced in *The Life of the Buddha* (Bangkok, 1958), pl. 24.

The Tempting of the Buddha and his Final Victory

The theme which the Thai refer to as "Buddha Subduing Māra" has some points in common with the Temptation of Christ, a subject not very frequently treated by the Western artist, who found greater scope for his imagination in the Temptation of Saint Anthony. This story, too, has many affinities with the Oriental myth.

In brief, the popular legend tells us that during the night in which the Enlightenment took place, but just before the Enlightenment, the meditating Sage, seated under a tree in the wilderness at the place now called Bodhgayā (near Patna), was approached by Māra, the Lord of the Realms of Desire. Māra was intent on preventing Prince Gotama from attaining Enlightenment, since anyone who reaches Nirvāna contributes to the depopulation of the Realms of Desire. Blandishments and seductions not succeeding, Māra used threats and summoned an immense army to subdue the obdurate Sage. The latter merely extended his right arm to touch the earth. Up rose the Earth Goddess, her long hair streaming with water. The water she wrung out of her hair was so profuse that it swept Māra and all his myriad hosts away. Its abundance is explained by the ancient Indian custom of pouring a libation of water on the soil every time one made a donation or agreed to a contract; he who was destined to be known as the Buddha had made so many donations in his previous lives that he was able, by touching the earth, to produce this spectacular result.

As stated thus, the theme is vastly simplified and may even be described as lacking in subtlety. In the canonical texts, and in the modified versions found in Sanskrit literature, Māra is the God of Desire and Death, whose power is directly threatened should Prince Gotama become the Buddha. He is alternately conceived in personal terms as an imp, a demon, or a God of Lust who has three daughters: Tanhā (Craving), Arati (Aversion) and Ragā (Passion). In addition he can assume a multitude of human forms. It is also possible to consider him in abstract terms exclusively, as a formulation of the "enemies within," such as Pride, Anger, Hypocrisy and all other obstacles to the attainment of Enlightenment.

Māra's assault on the meditating Sage is not a single event but a long succession of attacks assuming different aspects: taunts, promises, seductions, and threats. He is justified in his own eyes by the belief that he has achieved much greater merit than Gotama. The situation is rich with dramatic suspense; in the presence of an impassive figure, there is built up a crescendo which in the nature of things heightens the effects of the Buddha's final victory. A great victory it is indeed, which must account for the enormous popularity of this theme, especially in Thailand, where three out of four images of the seated Buddha one encounters show him performing the mudrā of *bhūmiśparsa*, or "touching the Earth."

Only painting can really do justice to a theme of such rich iconographic possibilities. Interesting examples may be found in various temples such as Wat Dusit in Tonburî and elsewhere, including several in Ayudhyā.

The painter has an advantage over the sculptor in that he can set a vast stage and literally populate it with a cast of thousands. As in the painting illustrated (Fig. 4), center stage must always be occupied by the meditating Sage. Given the episodic character of the story, which is supposed to take place in the course of one night but which could be stretched out in time, Māra and his minions, his daughters, his menacing demons, his evil spirits, his noxious beasts, and his myriad mercenaries in their full warlike accoutrements, can dart all over the picture space. Here the Earth Goddess occupies a central post below the Buddha while she wrings her hair to produce the flood which inundates all but the Sage and the righteous ones, who are witnessing the great event in the company of assorted guardians and angels. (Note that the artist has committed the iconographic error of making the Buddha touch the earth with his left hand.)

Sculptors have rarely tried to present the scene in all its complexity. No. 74 in the present exhibition may possibly represent such an attempt, but too many elements have been omitted for it to be very meaningful.

The figurine of the "Divinity of Terrifying Aspect," sometimes called the "Dancing Māra" (No. 32) also may have conceivably formed part of a discrete group composition illustrating the theme; if so, it would be a unique instance.[1] An isolated figure more frequently treated by sculptors

Fig. 5. The Earth Goddess Wringing Water from Her Hair. Bronze, H. 15⅛ in. (38.5 cm.). Bangkok Style, first half of the nineteenth century. National Museum, Bangkok.

is that of the Earth Goddess, Vasundhara, or Dharaṇī, as the Thai call her, who is usually shown in the attitude of wringing the water from her hair (Fig. 5).

The sculptor discovered very early that in order to convey the essential point of the theme he needs must concentrate on the main personage, and forget the episodic elements. What is that point? Obviously it is the Sage's superhuman strength of will in resisting every form of seduction and dire menace, of remaining serene and impassive in the midst of turbulence, and of subduing his tormentor with a gesture which is both authoritative and disdainful. It is in this latter respect that one may note a striking departure from the early canons, which describe the Sage's gesture in touching the earth below his right knee not as the almost casual act with which we are familiar, but as a smiting of the ground which causes the earth to roar and convulse itself in a frightening commotion.

The usual manner of depicting this event embodies a certain illogicality. According to the story, temptation takes place twice *before* the Enlightenment. All indications of halos or flames darting from the Sage's cranial protuberance (*ushnisha*) are, therefore, anticipatory symbols and in theory he should not even be referred to as the Buddha. In this exhibition only No. 15, a simple and almost naive image cast during the mid-Dvāravatī period, when Theravāda doctrine was presumably still uninfluenced by Mahāyāna practices, shows logical consistency: the Sage has no halo, and he sits on the plainest of grounds.[2] On the other hand, the great Śrīvijaya image known as the "Buddha of Grahi" (No. 30), which shows him seated on the coils of the Nāgarāja Mucalinda under the seven-headed cobra hood, enriches the legend by retroaction: this particular event took place six weeks after the Victory over Māra. One is almost led to believe that the victory is not a definitive one, that Māra perpetually keeps up his assault and that the Buddha must forever call the Earth Goddess to witness.

It is a tribute to the inherent genius of the various peoples who constituted Siam that in the course of more than a thousand years so many versions of "Buddha Subduing Māra" were created in such a variety of styles, of which the principal ones are well represented in this exhibition. Many of the works are of surpassing beauty; they most successfully convey the idea of an extraordinarily dignified and patient figure at a crucial moment in his life. "Grace Under Stress" might well serve as our Western equivalent for the Thai formula for the subject.

T. B.

For further discussion of this subject see Har Dayal, *The Bodhisattva Doctrine in Buddhist Sanscrit Literature* (London, 1932); Alfred Foucher, *La Vie du Bouddha* (Paris, 1949), pp. 142–178; O. C. Gangoly, "The Earth Goddess in Buddhist Art," *The Indian Historical Quarterly* 19 (1943): 1–11.

NOTES

1. Boisselier and Griswold believe that the title "Dancing Māra" used by the Bangkok Museum to describe this figure is inappropriate.

2. This opinion is based on the assumption that there never was a halo nor an elaborate pedestal for this piece. If Predestination is at work here then all iconographic anachronisms may be disregarded.

The Prince of Û Tòng

Rāmādhipati I, who established the kingdom of Ayudhyā in 1351, was born in 1314. His father was a man of obscure origin who made himself ruler of a place called Debanagara, which I believe should be indentified with Lopburî. The late Prince Damrong Rājanubhāb, renowned as a statesman, historian, and archaeologist, has shown that Rāmādhipati married the daughter of the Prince of Subarṇapurī and later, after inheriting the principality from him, became known as Prince of Û Tòng. As the name of a principality, Û Tòng and Subarṇapurī are doublets (both mean "place of gold"), but as present-day toponyms they are not. The present town of Subarnapurī is the capital of the homonymous province.

About 30 km. away is the town which, when Prince Damrong first went there in 1904, was called Jòraké Sâm Pan ("three thousand crocodiles"). He believed this was the earlier site of the capital of the principality, so (as Minister of the Interior) he changed it to Û Tòng.

Professor Boisselier's excavations at Jòraké Sâm Pan (Û Tòng) show that the site was abandoned in the eleventh century and not re-occupied until the seventeenth. Apparently the present town of Subarṇapurī was founded in the fifteenth century. We do not know where the capital of the principality was in the fourteenth century, though it cannot have been far away. Wherever it was, it was undoubtedly called Subarṇapurī or Subarṇabhūmi or Û Tòng, or all three interchangeably.

Rāmādhipati received another rich inheritance when his own father died in 1344. It was by consolidating his two inheritances that he founded the kingdom of Ayudhyā, for which he built a new capital at the present site of the city of that name. (See A. B. Griswold and Prasert ṇa Nagara, "King Lödaiya of Sukhodaya and his Contemporaries," Epigraphic and Historical Studies, no. 10, *Journal of the Siam Society* 60 [1972]:29–39.)

A. B. G.

The Buddha's Footprint

According to the Pali Commentarial literature the Buddha's height was 18 cubits (about nine yards), and his footsole was marked with 108 auspicious signs, the most prominent of which was the Wheel of the Doctrine.

Legend asserts that during the course of one of his miraculous visits to Ceylon he stamped the impression of his footsole in the rock on the summit of Adam's Peak. This Footprint, which is still visited by countless pilgrims, is described by Westerners as a shallow depression in the rock a little less than two yards long; the length would therefore be in just about the right proportion to the Buddha's height. Though the auspicious signs are no longer visible they are supposed to have been reproduced on a metal cover that protected the Footprint as late as the seventeenth century. The cover is now lost, but copies of it survive which display a diagram of the Footprint with the 108 signs on it.

The Footprint on Adam's Peak has been an object of intense veneration for centuries. Numerous copies of it, or rather of the metal cover, were installed in Southeast Asia for the benefit of persons who could not make a pilgrimage to Ceylon. The Footprint in our exhibition (No. 53) is one of these copies. Another one is referred to in an inscription composed in 1357 by King Mahādharmarājā I of Sukhodaya, who says that worshiping it is an act of merit that will bring the same advantages as worshiping the Buddha himself.

For a discussion of the 108 auspicious marks on such Footprints, see A. B. Griswold and Prasert ṇa Nagara, "The Inscription of Vằt Ṭrabāṅ Jāṅ Phöak," Epigraphic and Historical Studies, no. 7, *Journal of the Siam Society* 59 (1971):170–188.

A. B. G.

Selected Bibliography

ABBREVIATION:
JSS: Journal of the Siam Society

Anuman Rajadhon, Phya. "The Golden Meru." JSS 45, pt. 2 (1957): 65–71.
———. "Phra Cedi." JSS 40, pt. 1 (1952): 66–72.
Bidyalankarana, Prince. "The Buddha's Footprint." JSS 28, pt. 1 (1935): 1–14.
Boisselier, Jean. *La statuaire khmère et son évolution.* Saigon: 1955.
Buribhand, Luang Boribal and Griswold, A[lexander] B. "Sculpture of Peninsular Siam in the Ayudhyā Period." JSS 38, pt. 2 (1951): 1–60.
Briggs, Lawrence Palmer. *The Ancient Khmer Empire. Transactions of the American Philosophical Society*, n.s., vol. 41, pt. 1. Philadelphia: 1951.
Chand, M. C. E. and Yimsiri, Khien. *Thai Monumental Bronzes.* Bangkok: 1957.
Coedès, George. *Bronzes khmèrs.* Paris: 1923.
———. *Les collections archéologiques du Musée National de Bangkok. Ars Asiatica* 12 (1948).
———. *Les états hindouisés d'Indochine et d'Indonésie.* Paris: 1948.
———. "The Excavations at P'ong Tük and their Importance for the Ancient History of Siam." JSS 21, pt. 3 (1927–1928): 195–209.
———. *Pour mieux comprendre Angkor.* 2nd ed. rev. Paris: 1947.
Dhani Nivat, Prince. "The reconstruction of Rāma I of the Chakri Dynasty." JSS 43, pt. 2 (1955): 212–247.
Diskul, M. C. Subhadradis; Griswold, A[lexander] B.; Lyons, Elizabeth. *The Arts of Thailand.* Edited by Theodore Bowie. Bloomington, Indiana: 1960.
Döhring, K. *Kunst und Kunstgewerbe in Siam.* 3 vols. Berlin: n.d.
Dupont, Pierre. *L'archéologie mône de Dvāravatī.* Paris: 1959.
———. *La statuaire préangkorienne. Artibus Asiae*, Suppl. 15 (1955).
Feroci, C. "Aesthetics of Buddhist Sculpture." JSS 38, pt. 4 (1948): 39–46.
———. "Traditional Thai Painting." JSS 40, pt. 2 (1952): 147–155.
Fournereau, Lucien. *Le Siam ancien.* 2 vols. Paris: 1895–1908.
Griswold, A[lexander] B. *Dated Buddha Images of Northern Siam. Artibus Asiae*, Suppl. 16 (1957).
———. *Towards a History of Sukhodaya Art.* Bangkok: 1967.
Groslier, Bernard Philippe. *Indochina.* New York: 1966.
Hutchinson, E. W. "Sacred Images in Chiengmai." JSS 28, pt. 2 (1935): 115–142.
———. "The Seven Spires." JSS 39, pt. 1 (1951): 1–68.
La Loubère, Simon de. *A New Historical Relation of the Kingdom of Siam.* London: 1693.
———. *Du royaume de Siam.* Paris: 1691.
Le May, Reginald S. *A Concise History of Buddhist Art in Siam.* Cambridge: 1938.
———. *The Culture of South-East Asia.* London: 1954.
———. "A Visit to Sawankalok." JSS 19, pt. 2 (1925): 63–82.
Notton, C. *Annales du Siam.* 3 vols. Paris: 1926–1932.

Seidenfaden, Erick. "An Excursion to Lopburî." JSS 15, pt. 2 (1922): 66–77.

———. "An Excursion to Phimâi, a Temple City in the Khorat Province." JSS 17, pt. 1 (1923): 1–19.

Vliet, Jeremias van. "Description of the Kingdom of Siam." JSS 7, pt. 1 (1910): 1–105.

———. "Historical Account of Siam in the 17th century." JSS 30, pt. 2 (1938): 95–154.

Wales, H. G. Quaritch. *Dvāravatī: The Earliest Kingdom of Siam*. London: 1969.

———. "The Origins of Sukhodaya Art." JSS 44, pt. 2 (1956): 113–124.

Wells, Kenneth E. *Thai Buddhism, its Rites and Activities*. Bangkok: 1939.

Woods, W. A. R. *A History of Siam*. 2nd ed. Bangkok: 1933.

Designed by Bert Clarke
Composition by A. Colish, Mount Vernon, N.Y.
Production supervised by John Weatherhill, Inc.,
New York and Tokyo
Printed in gravure and lithography by
Nissha Printing Co. Ltd., Kyoto